Facing Forwards
Europe. Solo. No Looking Back.

First published: 2016
Copyright © 2016 Lorraine Wilson

For more copies, please email: **whistlebooks@gmail.com**

Typeset by **Chris Collins**
Illustration © **Kirk Houston 2016**
Cover design by **@LoneWolf_72**
Printed by **Bell and Bain, Glasgow**

ISBN   978-0-9935079-0-8

eISBN   978-0-9935079-1-5

FACING
FORWARDS

EUROPE. SOLO.
NO LOOKING BACK.

LORRAINE WILSON

FOR

Dad, who taught me the value of getting away from it all.
Rusty Qui, who taught me the value of never giving up.
Sparkly. Without you the book would have been considerably shorter.

Thanks

To Steve Davie, who didn't want me to go but was with me in spirit
every step of the way and to Dawn Bartlett, who made me think the
journey was as brave as the first Moon landing.

To friends old and new who shared part of the journey – Sonja and
Mekki Abel, Ulrike and Jana Herost, Sarah Topps and Mark Fayers,
Robert Haddock and Steve Botting, John McKellar, the Clark family
(Stew, Elaine, Aidan and Adam), Helma van der Brink, Marija Pavleska,
Leonardo Montagni, the Huddersfield boys, and many others…

To Mike and Vicky for keeping me on my feet.

Special thanks to my talented friends who helped me put *Facing
Forwards* together. Linda Isles for editing, the Lone Wolf for jacket
and photo page design, Kirk Houston for illustration, Chris Collins for
typesetting, Ewan Smith for formatting the e-book, and an extra special
thanks to Matthew Marra who shared his font genius and love of a
striking graphic to give the initial Crowdfunder campaign such
a strong visual identity.

CONTENTS

BEFORE
WE GO

EVERYTHING that follows is true.

The idea was a straightforward one. Travel Europe for three months by train, visiting as many countries as possible. From the beginning the most important aspect of the journey was to do it alone.

At that point there was no book. It was a decision to take a break from life. A life that hasn't been particularly cruel but the previous five years had been draining in the extreme. Years of financial meltdown, heartbreak, poor health, and an almighty lack of direction had accumulated in an overwhelming realisation that things had to change.

There were moments of joy of course, but they were becoming less frequent and always dependent on events. The next gig, the next comedy show; whatever would distract me from the reality of the day-to-day.

For example, my lifestyle was increasingly unhealthy. After more than a decade of having dogs, two had gone to pooch heaven and a third was now living with my ex. Long walks without a dog were too upsetting. Consequently, the furthest I walked was to the driver's side of the car.

Comfort eating and wine consumption had become the norm. Things had been miserable but believe me, no-one needs that much comfort. And with every doughnut and every glass of Merlot, every ounce of self-confidence that had managed to hang on in there was smothered in fat and sugar and drowned in alcohol.

Freelance writing, even the relatively successful kind, had become more of a hamster wheel than a career, so it was time to stop. For once say no – and stop. Stopping didn't mean sitting in a chair and watching sunsets. Stopping meant that I could keep moving in a completely different way.

There was an opportunity for a new life – the offer of a job in Abu Dhabi later in the year, so the prospect of spending rather than earning for three months was not particularly frightening. The sale of my house had gone through so there was something of a financial cushion. I had no home, I was living with a friend, and had sold or given away all of my possessions apart from three suitcases full of clothes and keepsakes. To my mind this was the greatest opportunity I would ever have to take off and see if travelling could teach me as much as I always thought it might.

The reaction to the decision to travel solo was surprising. Not exactly negative, but puzzled and often appalled from some quarters. From others it was a reaction bordering on envy. Actually let's stay truthful, it was full-blown jealousy that someone could take the decision to just go, and go it alone. Not that they would ever do it – there was something of escape by proxy.

The most common question was 'Why?' The instant response was 'Why not?' However, the more people asked me, the more I asked myself, and putting it down on paper seemed to be the answer. Just because I was breaking out of the hamster cage didn't mean I should stop doing what I loved.

To gauge interest in a book on the journey, a Crowdfunder campaign to cover the production of the first run was mounted, and it was successful. It looked like the idea of the journey had touched a nerve.

The fact that so many people had faith in what I could deliver did add pressure to deliver an exciting read. From the beginning the decision was to be completely truthful – manufacturing drama is lying to a reader, lying to myself, and would be disrespectful to the sincere significance of other events.

Three months in any life will have highs and lows; there will be periods of frantic activity and others when it feels that time is standing still. And so it was here, but amplified. The highs were euphoric and overwhelming, the lows were crushing and almost unbearable. There is no doubt that I had to be sharper – every sense and instinct was more acute, but there were moments of beautiful stillness, usually when there was nothing to do but wait for the train to rumble its way to the next destination through endless countryside.

Sometimes to feel the thrill of the rollercoaster, we need to get aboard the mini-train, as mundane or annoying as that can be.

It's tempting to leave out specific events that will tie the journey to summer 2015 but, as I hope you'll see, some had an unequivocal effect on how I felt about a time or a place.

Planning the trip, the idea was to escape and have minimal contact with home. That was really stupid. Of course there were outside pressures from home, but without that contact staying the course would have been much more difficult – in fact I wouldn't have made it.

But I did. Sorry to spoil the ending, but the fact that I did was perhaps the most life-changing aspect of the journey – and there were many.

The decision about what the book would be could not be made until the end of the journey of course. It isn't a straightforward travel book; there are no 'Top Ten Places to get a Mojito in Bucharest', but there was a desire to get outside of Europe's main destinations and look for the unusual. It isn't a self-help book, but if anyone finds a smidgeon of inspiration, it will be a massive bonus. It isn't a memoir but while writing the inclusion of earlier life events proved helpful in providing context to a particularly momentous event, or were added simply because they might be entertaining. Or not. When those are recent and personal, names will be left out. Not knowing names won't detract from the substance, please trust me.

With no expectations from a publisher about which section of the reading public this could be marketed to, there was a genuine freedom to tell the story sincerely. Like the journey, as the book went on I felt less and less inclined to play it safe.

Having to do everything a publisher normally would added to the pressure, but the idea of taking the book through from inception to having the honestly written, hopefully inspirational book in a reader's hands appealed enormously. Another challenge.

My hope is that this book will have the same effect as the moment when a traveller takes their suitcase from the luggage and unzips it to reveal the contents. It's almost impossible not to have a peek.

Having talented friends who I could employ to edit, design, typeset, and illustrate helped of course, but whether it succeeded or failed was always in my hands. If the book is in your hands and you don't know me, I'll chalk that one up as a win.

Like any journey, you've started at the beginning. You're also travelling solo. Let's meet up at the end.

Lorraine

THE
JOURNEY

He who is outside his door already has the
hardest part of his journey behind him.

Dutch proverb

ON THAT LAST day of May, passengers waiting to board the Eurostar from London to Brussels were the customary jumble of humanity.

There were young parents trying to corral toddlers using the bribery of the juice box, mouths fixed in a grinning rictus that would be remedied by the first beer of the trip.

Standing quite still were the anxious travellers; those who would break into a flurry of sudden activity, to check that their passport or ticket hadn't disappeared since the last check five minutes before.

There were the shuffling suits, complete with the professional baggage of a business traveller, resigned to another continental commute; their hearts at a family Sunday dinner while they prepared for a night in the company flat with nothing more than a pizza and too much wine.

There was also a deeply religious woman who, having had little traction with many in the queue, moved on to a lost soul in a rain jacket, cap, and backpack, clearly ripe for a quick conversion between check-in and boarding.

I told her to bugger off. I did. Not immediately of course.

The *thank you but I'm not interested* approach was having no effect. As my indifference mounted her fervour grew, and it was only when I joined the ranks of anxious passengers, checking my waist pack once again, that she grasped my arm and said God would be with me on my journey.

Without replying that I hoped not – the whole point was to do this thing alone, I removed her claw from my forearm. Then I told her to bugger off.

She was clearly used to it as, without missing a beat, she moved smoothly on to a tall Dutch woman who I had pegged as a former Olympic figure skater. It was a long wait in this queue and imagination can help to pass the time.

It was time to check the waist pack again. A passport, wallet, Interrail pass, mobile phone, and a few ginger chews to help with motion sickness. The idea of facing forwards wasn't only symbolic. When my back is to travel, motion sickness is a certainty.

Despite the throng, mine seemed to be the solitary backpack – enough to single out a budget traveller if my designed-for-comfort outfit wasn't. However, with only 40L of space to carry everything required for three months, it wasn't bulky enough to send anyone flying by turning sideways too quickly.

Paring the load down to essentials had been inspired by journalist Nellie Bly who, in 1889, took nothing more than a bag measuring 16 inches wide by seven inches high on a journey where she circumnavigated the globe in 72 days in her successful attempt to beat Phileas Fogg's 80 days in Jules Verne's tale.

Wearing one dress, tailored to withstand the rigours of the journey, one coat, and one hat, her bag had underwear, cold cream, paper, pen and ink, a hip flask, nightwear, and a tennis blazer. Quite a woman.

While I edited the contents of my backpack at the flat of my friend Dawn, she marvelled at how ruthless I had become. Not a minimalist by nature, she shook her head at items discarded as unnecessary, then offered me a procession of items of clothing that she felt I needed to take – each one was more beautiful and stylish than anything I owned, but far from necessary.

If contact lenses were being left behind as a luxury item, then a designer skirt with intricate beading was not taking their place. If an old laptop was being discarded as too heavy, then a pair of heavy black leather boots weren't making up that weight. This backpack would be a mobile home for three months – not exactly feather light but not heavy enough to cause any major strains. Any small souvenirs, notebooks, tickets, and leaflets would be posted back.

This minimalism was heady stuff. In my zeal to travel light and make some significant changes in my life, hefty walking shoes were discarded in favour of sandals. Granny sandals for sure, but with an ethnic twist. Not a bold move for most, but for an individual with a strong aversion to bare feet, even her own, it was a bit of a breakthrough. Ten years ago this was tackled during a course of Cognitive Behavioural Therapy, but it was time to put the theory into practice.

In the backpack was another item of similarly skimpy footwear that would also expose all 10 toes to the air. That final day of May brought those unsuspecting toes rain. Lots of rain.

Those final preparations in London included a travel alarm to save draining the phone of charge; a lightweight plastic dinner service comprising plate, bowl, mug, and cutlery; and the essential inflatable neck pillow.

There was nothing to buy that could counter the sudden feeling of being completely unprepared, however. With an Interrail pass for the next month and two nights booked in the spare room of a Belgian teacher through Airbnb, nothing else was planned. With no-one to consult along the way my decisions, for good or bad, could only lie at one set of already soggy sandals.

Following the final ticket checks it was time to get on board. During those checks my potential saviour was addressed as Sister. Great, I hadn't even left the UK and had already sworn at a nun. It was the bad fire for me. Or bad karma. Whatever, it wasn't good.

On board and approving of the low-key upholstery choice, the backpack straps were folded away in a zipped compartment for fear that their dangling might offend fellow passengers.

And as the train departed, I was simply overwhelmed at what was about to happen, even though what that was wasn't at all clear. There was no real sense of excitement.

My view was obscured by the racing raindrops and the countryside with its particular Sunday bleakness. This was Morrissey weather but it was far too early for ennui. At that point I was grateful the iPod had made the baggage cut and I had the sense to take it from the backpack before settling into my window seat. My neighbour somehow managed to fall asleep as soon as she sat down and was now sleep burbling in French.

Headphones on, in case I somehow managed to understand something too personal that she said in this vulnerable state, there was no way to choose the perfect soundtrack. Song shuffle it had to be, but as in every other moment of emotional fragility every lyric was imbued with greater significance than it would have had at any other time.

It had been three months since I left my tidy white cottage in Dundee. I had closed the door and put it on the market with no regret. It was a home that, like almost every other, had seen wonderfully happy times, moments of despair, and the inevitable humdrum. It would be another three months before I was back in Dundee, and only for a short time before moving to work in Abu Dhabi.

The significance of that next three months hit home and with each subsequent song, the gut-churning escalated. Before the tears came it was time to pack it away. But only when my neighbour had woken up.

Any faint hope of emerging from the tunnel into a sunny French evening were dashed when the raindrops gave as good chase as the British. Being back in mobile phone signal land, there were a few messages from the host of the Airbnb room asking about arrival time, which had already been discussed, but hey…pas de problème. I was feeling more European already.

The choice of accommodation in Brussels had come down to the suitability of the owner, ruling out any who looked as if they might have a dungeon, any that were too pricey, and any too far from the station.

The host provided instructions of how to reach the flat from Bruxelles Midi, without pinpointing which of the numerous exits to use. From the map, however, my home for the next two nights was minutes away.

Forty minutes later, the backpack finally came to rest in the clean, comfortable room where my host provided a key before heading into the Brussels evening – probably to sit at a pavement café and discuss philosophy while drinking and smoking; but in an intellectual way.

As she floated away like an effortlessly stylish pixie, I tried to dry out my sandals and investigated how much damage a ponytail band had done to my hair. Too much to repair that evening it seemed, but it was after 8pm and time to find food.

Like many major cities, the area around the railway station attracts not only the unfortunate but those who make the other side of the street appear more attractive. The looks I was receiving that night made me wonder in which category they were putting me. True, I was dressed for comfort and to disguise my bulk, but there's no way that sandals, a baseball cap, ill-fitting grey joggers, and a blue rainproof jacket was a threatening look. It must have been the first.

Anywhere that provided a warming evening meal would be acceptable. Anywhere. Except the first dozen places dotted along Boulevard Maurice Lemonnier, all rejected for equally spurious reasons. It was important to get this one right. It would be the first meal of the trip and had to be memorable for the **right** reasons.

A step in one puddle too many made a small and unassuming restaurant the one. It was empty but the sign outside promised poulet et frites. What could possibly go wrong with chicken and chips? Half of the dish the Belgians invented anyway – not the chicken. The owner was so surprised to see a customer that his ashtray was swatted off the table. The cook, who had been sitting chatting, darted back into the open kitchen.

With a sit anywhere shrug, he suggested a table for two in the middle of the room and asked if I would like something to drink, in French, which pleased me. Despite all outward appearances saying textbook tourist, I was able to answer him in phrasebook tourist, which appeared to please him equally.

My choice of beer, he said, was for the tourists (I bet he says that to all the tourists) and so I suggested he bring me something that would complement the roast chicken. The beer arrived with the meal, which was memorable for not being terrible. It was beer so golden that it brought a little sun. An examination of the label revealed that it was (ahem) only 9% ABV, something that brought a whack of warmth to accompany the sun.

The walk back had a sway, the lights along the boulevard had a twinkle, the puddle paddling didn't feel quite so horrific, and what followed was a solid night of sleep in a bed that I didn't remember being quite so close to the ground.

The host had already left the apartment by the time I came to. Throwing back the curtains it was good news. The sun had arrived and there would be no shoe shopping for Wellington boots today. Would they call them that here, this being Waterloo territory?

Buoyed by the weather, it was straight into the shower with a handy space-saving shampoo sachet. Too fiddly to open with wet hands, I gave it a yank with my teeth and it yielded, along with one of my teeth.

A crown had become dislodged, fallen out, and was heading towards the drain like a canoeist too close to the edge of the falls. Even in the panic, it was saved from the big drop. My tongue explored what felt like a mouth chasm, too close to the front for comfort. The first day. The first bloody day.

Assessing the scale of the dental disaster in the mirror, a gap had opened up that meant full-on smiles were impossible without frightening children, and I certainly wouldn't smile at anyone near the railway station for fear that they would cross the road. Also there, on my top lip, was a fully blown cold sore that really should have had its own Eurostar ticket.

Having heard horrific tales about the cost of dental treatment from friends living in Europe, the morning began with the search for an Apotheek to find something, anything, that could be a temporary fix. The assistant looked on with some pity but could offer nothing but a temporary fixative for dentures.

One thing was perhaps more surprising than the moment when I heard the crack and felt the tooth making its escape – how unconcerned I was. Normally doing something this daft would have been followed by intense self-loathing, but in this situation, unless I went straight home, I had to get on with it.

A traditional petit déjeuner outside a tourist trap at the Grand Place restarted the day with a little more sophistication, and a glass of orange juice as expensive (5 Euros, 10 cents) as the waiter was offhand.

There had been mixed reviews of Brussels before the trip, from the sublime to the downright dull. For me, this was the first stop in a three-month European odyssey. Brussels was seen through eyes that were excited to be seeing anything new, and they saw pleasing things.

Avoiding the parliament and its politics, Brussels is a city to stroll. It's expansive enough for a leg stretch, but so compact that public transport isn't necessary to explore its heart, with wider boulevards and winding cobbled streets intermingling. Window shopping in the Galleries Royal St Hubert avoided a brief shower. There was a real freedom about travelling light and knowing that actual shopping wasn't an option.

High above the city, the lack of any meaningful research or preparation became apparent when chancing upon the Palace of Brussels and realising that Belgium had a monarchy. The tone was set for the journey, however, when no photographs of the grand palace were taken, but many of a bus heading to Wiener were.

This part of the city was quieter, with runners making the most of the park opposite the palace. The crowds near the Grand Place, at the corner of Stoofstraat and Eikstraat, might have been an indication of something worthwhile. Approaching tentatively I feared a street performer, but the camera blur and selfie stick frenzy was for the Mannekin Pis, a small bronze statue of a boy peeing. It's as underwhelming as it sounds.

The morning's dental debacle had taken some of the shine off the day but nothing that would have made a genuinely interesting sight any less so. A small bronze boy taking a whizz was not that. The fear of a falling tooth did dampen any enthusiasm to communicate though. The fixative stuck the tooth to the inside of my lip, so trying to talk curled my lip into an Elvis sneer.

It wasn't a hardship. Being alone has never been a problem. In the past there would be days on end when I would speak to no-one but the dogs, who certainly responded to my voice, but there was a lack of witty repartee.

It also had an impact on dining decisions, but it was a fine evening to sit at a street stall. Not being a seafood eater the local dish of moules were out, but the frites were fine. This time it was a generous cone of golden, piping hot, fluffy, chunky loveliness from the stall on Rue de la Madeleine, topped with sweet mayonnaise and accompanied by another Belgian beer. My choice this time – a lightweight 5%.

On the next table, a group of young guys were being loud and probably on their third or fourth beer when a police car pulled up and its burly occupants headed straight for them. It seemed a tad excessive until they gave the boys a high five and walked past to pick up their own frites to eat in the car.

The backstreets were quiet and yielded occasional surprises, such as the Jacques Brel museum, but this was the point in the day when it struck me that the next day was open to me. Where to go? How would I get there? Where would I sleep?

In the end, on the first day of European travelling, the Interrail pass wouldn't get too much of a workout. The next stop was to be Bruges, only an hour and 20 minutes away to the west but a destination that had been on the outskirts of my understanding for many years. One night should be enough if I arrived mid-morning. With that early start, I bumped into my host.

The night before she had obviously been in a philosophy professor's apartment, listening to Brel while being ravishing but also wise and quoting her own poetry. Forgetting that the escaped tooth hadn't been attached yet and the cold sore was still at the height of its powers, I smiled warmly. She recoiled, clearly wondering how this leprous, snaggle-toothed old crone had got through the vetting process. She bade me farewell, clearly thinking that three days on the rails might be too much for me, never mind three months.

I'm lazy. But it's the lazy people who invented the wheel and the bicycle because they didn't like walking or carrying things.

Lech Walesa

DESPITE HAVING SEEN *In Bruges*, which placed Colin Farrell in the town as a hitman on the run, the name Bruges still had the ring of elderly women on two-centre bus tours, coupling the canals of Bruges and the Dutch bulb fields; a place trimmed in lace. Without too much further investigation a hotel was booked at an admittedly cool address of t'Zand in what was described as the historical centre.

At the station, I dutifully filled out the travel report part of the pass as advised in the Interrail information booklet. Then checked it. And again. And again.

Across the aisle, once I had finished taking in the Belgian hipster opposite, I turned my attention to a young couple working through a large bag of nuts with a set of nutcrackers – each. They were backpackers too, but I had user-friendly bananas and baby cheeses. I wondered what had been discarded to allow nutcrackers to make the baggage cut, until I saw that they were also carrying a large brick of Parmesan and a fancy grater. No doubt the kitchen sink was in there for hand washing.

Outside, the journey was uninspiring with flat countryside and small stations, but Bruges arrived quickly and the challenge to locate that night's accommodation began. After wandering aimlessly for a few minutes, adjusting the backpack for comfort and deciding the chest straps were too bondage-like for a girl with my plentiful frontage, the task couldn't be avoided.

Most people were heading in the same direction, so it seemed wise to tag on to the back of a crowd who were happy to flash their maps in public and know where they were going – as opposed to my approach. It took a measly 15 minutes to reach that historical centre, through film set streets and cobbled lanes.

Realising that I probably wasn't staying in the same hotel as these oblivious guides, I peeled off from the pack and made an attempt at finding my hotel. I was there. The street sign said so. It was a small shopping street, currently being re-cobbled, with the roadworks taking a fair bit of negotiation in sandals.

Several lengths of the street later, it was clear that the hotel didn't exist. I had even resorted to the map, twisting and turning it to get some point of orientation. Day two and I hadn't just lost a tooth, I'd been scammed by an online booking site. What was to become of me?

At one point, with sore feet and wet through from a sudden shower, my head finally went down. And there it was. In front of an anonymous white building, the name of the tiny hotel was marked on the pavement – ideal for those visitors who prefer to avoid looking up.

The room was at the top with a view of the territory I had covered with such intensity for the past hour or so. An early check-in allowed drying time and, despite the dallying delay, it was only lunchtime.

Back on the street and heading further into the centre, there was a creeping realisation that Bruges was an excellent idea. The beginning of June was too early for the main tourist season, but that meant the streets were quiet and it was possible to wander canal side without much hindrance.

Of all the picture postcard houses, one stood out. It was more modern than the rest and not painted in a traditional colour – a warm white with a light blue trim. There was an open gate and a tiny courtyard so I had a peek, always loving a nice courtyard.

For all I knew the owners were hovering behind the curtains, wondering why a woman wearing sandals in the rain was staring at their home, and wondering whether they should call the police.

It was one of those *what if?* moments that every traveller experiences. In this particular vision I, effortlessly stylish, was on a bicycle and pedalling languorously enough to let two Jack Russell Terriers trot along beside me. Everything was fantasy, but one thing in particular. The ability to ride a bicycle.

They had been evident in Brussels, but in Bruges the two-wheeled terrors were king. And at least cars had to stay on the road. Cyclists, even furnished with generous lanes, liked to mount the pavement believing pedestrians had a sixth sense about when and where to move. The alternative was a collision with a wicker panier.

When it happened, the best way to handle this mild peril seemed to be to stand still. With little confidence as a driver and no cycling skills at all, it seemed that even my long and impressive track record as a pedestrian was being called into question.

Reaching Jan Van Eyck Square, there appeared to be a few victims of the wicked cyclists, lying on the ground. On closer examination, they were protected from the wet cobbles by a low box painted in bright orange. When they left, I circled it like a small child not knowing whether she can take a biscuit from a plate without permission.

Taking the risk, I reclined until flat with my face feeling the joy of weak sun. Through my body was a rush of, well it wasn't quite clear then, but it was marvellous – a pleasant tingle the likes of which can be enjoyed alone, but not in the open air without risking arrest. A plaque on the side of the box said this was Brugge Tuned, where the traffic noise was converted in real time into harmonic vibrations and fed through the box. Traffic was good for something then. I shut my eyes then tuned into the city and out of everything else.

It wasn't long before black clouds reappeared and with them the rain that sploshes rather than drops. It was time to seek shelter. My fondness for the Belgian way with a potato was rewarded by chancing upon the Frietmuseum. Housed in an impressive building, it was a temple to the tattie, a champion of the chip, a must-see for all fans of the friet, which is the Belgian spelling. No detail escaped the displays and arty installations of potato loveliness. There was also the inside scoop on how Belgium is the real birthplace of the snack food that American soldiers are responsible for naming French Fries.

With displays of salty saucy advertising and vintage equipment for getting those frites perfect, there is also some startling frite-themed statuary and, of course, a café to try out the fellas themselves. Not a patch on Brussels the night before, but knowing sacrilege when I hear it I delivered an empty tray and headed back towards the hotel.

There was only one more stop to make – a shoe shop. The sandals might have been built for comfort, but with unpredictable weather a pair of good walking shoes (rather like the ones sitting in London actually) were required.

Most shops lining the street towards the invisible hotel looked, at first, as if they sold footwear found in a pamphlet that falls from an elderly relative's reading material. Close to the hotel, a window had the attraction of a SALE and, in one small corner, a selection of shoes for the under 80s.

One pair of Timberland walking shoes later, it was back to the sanctuary of the attic room and time to plan my next move. It was clear that the first part of the journey would be a case of learning on the job. The sleepless night was not only down to the wild storm that blustered and whistled, but the realisation this was perhaps a bigger task than I had imagined.

Between the decision to make the journey and heading off, which was a few weeks, there had been no time to plan a definite route. There was a general direction in mind, but the Interrail pass should provide flexibility, and being able to book accommodation online meant I shouldn't have to turn up anywhere with nowhere to sleep.

The storm passed through the night and the morning was calm and clear. The plan was to get to Rotterdam by evening so there was time to see Bruges under this blue sky. The journey was only two and a half hours, so a quick stop in Antwerp, close to the Dutch border, was also possible.

Breakfast was included in the room rate so it was time to get my buffet on. A deep love affair with continental breakfast began on a school holiday to Switzerland in 1980. With a coach from Dundee to the Bernese Oberland, there was a stop overnight in Germany – Heidelberg to be precise. Morning brought a breakfast with crusty rolls in the shape of flowers and, were we seeing things? Chocolate? In spreading form? For breakfast? To a 13-year-old with a sweet tooth, Germany became the greatest country on the planet.

Full of continental goodies, I had a few more hours to spend in Bruges. This was the chance to send back the first package of notes, receipts, postcards, and other items that would jog my memory when it came to writing. With no laptop, writing notes longhand and keeping every ticket and flyer became crucial.

The post office was in Grote Markt, which the day before had been a grey, cold, deserted square. This morning, under sunny skies, the people of Bruges were out in force at a market selling food, flowers, and household goods.

The post office was quiet, but on approaching the counter, I was shooed away. Standing in space, clearly clueless, there followed some elaborate pointing to a machine. It was necessary to take a number and wait to be called. I looked around, gestured at the invisible crowds, and she shrugged. The beckoning beep came and I walked forward and handed her the number with a quizzical scowl. She shrugged again. *It's just how it works*, she said.

There was time for a slow dander around the gorgeous town square and to light a few candles in the Basilica of the Holy Blood for those friends who would appreciate it. I don't have a religious faith and believe churches are only attractions for those who do. It had the overwrought interior of most Catholic places of worship, primarily reminding us how sinful we are. After lighting the candles, it was only right to sit for a moment and think about family and friends who were having a tough time. There was a tiny tear, but it was the music. Honestly.

Everything was packed and ready to go at the hotel. The mobile phone had been charging and was now fully juiced, but as the European power adaptor was pulled from the wall, one pin decided it would rather stay in Bruges. It was useless now, so this charge would have to suffice until I arrived in Rotterdam where there would be shops. I knew that much.

At the station storage containers had sprung up, with an offer painted on the side to *Become A New Citizen Of Bruges*. It was a combination of art project and social survey, asking visitors how they would like to live in the city. Thinking back to the cream house with the blue trim and the distinct lack of lavender-smelling tour groups buying lace, answering the questions was easy.

Antwerp was fewer than 90 minutes away. With, I reckoned, four hours here, I ambled along the platform and became slack-jawed as the station began to reveal itself.

Some buildings are extravagant for the sake of excess, built during times of a city's great wealth to show its position in the world. This is true of Antwerp Central Station, but somehow it manages to be overblown with taste. The light and the sense of scale means that even with hundreds of people using the concourse, there was an aura of peace.

Using instinct to choose destinations as opposed to research was paying off so far. I loved Antwerp and hadn't stepped outside the station.

With a free map in hand from tourist information and the backpack resting in a luggage locker, the incredible euphoria that comes with a new city was unmistakable. The accommodation in Rotterdam had been booked for that night, but this could certainly be a recce for a return visit.

The station square had the tempting prospect of Antwerp Zoo, but this was the condensed version. In the middle distance, beyond the station square, there were the glinting gates that announce a city's Chinatown. Following the freedom to roam in Bruges, apart from bicycles of course, there was another threat to survival here, this time tram-shaped. Trams are wonderful, but for the stranger it can be difficult to judge their intended direction and speed of approach, bringing me to a halt for five minutes or so while locals wandered over the intricate web of tram lines while texting, bending down to tie shoelaces, picking up their dog's poop...

Hanging on the back of a particularly confident pensioner I made it and had soon reached Chinatown. In truth it turned out to be more of a

Chinahamlet with a couple of streets of relevant restaurants and shops, but not the bustling, evocative atmosphere I had hoped for.

Antwerp has a more commercial feel than Brussels. The map guided me towards Meir, a wide pedestrianised shopping street where it was tempting to look for a new charger, but there was limited time here.

At ground level, it was a street that can be seen through much of Europe, albeit with more than a sprinkling of designer temples, but above is where Antwerp's history as a rich trading port shows in the architecture. Build it higher, build it bigger – then they'll know we're important. The cathedral is so tall, at 404ft, a Japanese tourist toppled backwards trying to fit the entire spire into his viewfinder. This happened in one of the cobbled squares that were packed with tour groups, reminding me of a favourite rainy afternoon film from my childhood, *If It's Tuesday, This Must Be Belgium*, where a group of American tourists embark on a European coach tour through nine countries in 18 days. It was Wednesday, but the tour leader holding an umbrella aloft and the group, happy to follow and absolve all responsibility for their own happiness, was familiar, and not just from the film.

Heading back to the station, there was a welcome sighting of two chirpy Jack Russell Terriers and a busker who specialised in a game of *Name That Tune*. Fascinated that the tune couldn't be named after more than a minute, I stopped. Maybe being stationary would help. It didn't. In the end the chorus revealed that it was ABBA's *Fernando* – inside his head anyway.

Taking time to explore the station again, it was as impressive in its modernity with its double-decker tracks. I knew Rotterdam was only an hour away and I was excited, it being my first visit there. The Swiss school trip had taken the Hull to Rotterdam ferry, but our bus had driven straight through the Netherlands. That trip was on my mind as a group of teenagers barrelled through the carriage with a few adults, obviously teachers, in tow. They were boisterous but good-natured and it was surprising how the noise didn't grate as much because I didn't know what they were saying. Perhaps it's the content of loud chatter rather than the volume that's a problem.

I wondered how fellow passengers must have reacted to a group of Dundonian schoolchildren on that ferry, away from home with friends, and their teachers at a discreet distance. There were no smartphones to keep us quiet.

After a few minutes the teenagers settled, reached into bags and pockets for their phones and stared into the screens for the remainder of the journey, sometimes glancing to one another and giggling at silent messages passing between them. Plus ça change, plus c'est la même chose eh?

The more I travelled, the more I realised that fear
makes strangers of people who should be friends.

Shirley MacLaine (Don't Fall Off The Mountain)

IT WAS DIFFICULT to leave Rotterdam station, not due to the exquisite architecture, but because there were ticket barriers – and I had no ticket that could scan. It was clearly a common occurrence for the guard who produced a card with a QR code before I opened my mouth. The backpack said it all.

Taking no chances, I asked if this was the best exit for Weena, where that night's accommodation was located, and he nodded. It wasn't. After 20 minutes of witless wandering I headed back through the station, left through the front entrance, then stood back in awe. If Antwerp station was an indication of where the city had been, Rotterdam station was space age in comparison and an almighty welcome to the city.

Weena runs pretty much directly from the station concourse, so this would be no problem at all. The issue was that the photograph on the booking app resembled nothing along this stretch of road. Where was the traditional B&B in this road of modern office blocks and shops?

I had enough charge and mobile data to remind myself of the actual address (not a bad idea to check that) but arriving at the number, it was a modern apartment block. The name of the hotel was written in tiny letters against a buzzer, so there was little to be done but buzz.

Instructed to take the lift to the fourth floor, my host waited at the door of an apartment. This was a portal from modern Rotterdam to a Russian brothel. The small apartment was claustrophobic and packed with ornate furniture rarely seen outside of an amusement arcade window display. Only the giant ceramic leopard was missing.

Over two levels, the ground floor had a lounge where the gentleman of the house, sporting a particularly historic vest, reclined on a bottle green leather sofa watching TV. Beyond that was what used to be a balcony, now with the outside world screened off by vertical blinds and accommodating a double bed and several items of office equipment. In the tiny kitchen an insistent Japanese woman with a child hanging off each leg pointed to a mug and repeated the word COFFEE with increasing volume. She was ignored by the host, who in these surroundings looked straight from central casting for the brothel keeper. If I hadn't already paid (and it hadn't been so cheap), I would have turned and ran, but this Cynthia Payne of the Urals was intriguing.

It was unlikely that the shops would still be open to furnish me with an adaptor, but it was worth a try and looking for another bed would have eaten into that already limited time. Still ignoring the pleading for a cup of Java, the hostess showed me to the first floor and my room. The blown wallpaper took at least six inches from its length and breadth. There were twin beds, a dresser, a large television, several chairs, and a coffee table. There was, however, no floor space. Cats could visit happily, with no fear of being swung. The décor continued the downstairs theme. If I could be photographed on the bed in a bikini and touting a Kalashnikov, the picture would be at home on any Russian brides website.

Behind the twin beds there appeared to be a balcony hidden behind vertical blinds and heavy curtains. This could be accessed by pushing the headboard of one bed forward, sucking everything in, turning sideways, and squeezing through the gap.

The shared bathroom was a riot of burgundy with a toilet designed for toddlers and a bathroom mirror with multi-coloured disco lights. I shared this level with the caffeine-deprived Japanese lady and her children, who liked to shout.

There was little to keep me here. I headed back along Weena to the shopping area but had missed the shopping hours. The phone was now dead so there was no possibility of planning any journeys or making accommodation bookings for the next day. Around the main shopping area it was also difficult to find a place to eat. With the shops closed it was slightly Dystopian, as if the only thing to survive the apocalypse would be cockroaches feasting on the food of the golden arches.

There had been a solemn self-promise not to frequent any of the usual chains. It appeared to be the only option but no, there were supermarkets. Supermarkets are one of the great fascinations when abroad and they're everywhere – usually. It took an hour to find Dirk, a supermarket rather than a new boyfriend, but armed with a pre-packaged salad and a ready mixed shandy, the balcony awaited. Manoeuvring past the headboard I congratulated myself for making it on to the balcony, which was also overlooked by the Japanese family. One of the urchins poked his head through the net curtains and stared. And stared and stared. I stared back. I stared back hard.

I was tired and hungry and traumatised that this Caesar Salad was 80% cold potato, so I did what any 48-year-old would. I stuck out my tongue at him, at precisely the moment his mother came to drag him away from the window.

Retreating, there was little else to do but watch TV until it was time to sleep. The relic fired up with the whoosh of a jet engine and opened with Russia's Greatest Mysteries. It had subtitles. It would do.

The morning began with a purpose. Having beaten my neighbours to the disco bathroom, next on the list was Mission Adaptor. Having to check out at 11am, there wouldn't be too much time to power up for the next stage of the journey, and I wanted to spend as much of it in Rotterdam as possible.

Cynthia was a little perturbed that I didn't want breakfast. She was blocking the front door, which was disturbing, but with a promise that she could feed me on my return I was allowed to leave.

The tourist information office seemed like the natural place to ask for advice on where to buy such a thing. Apart from charging 1 Euro 50 for a city map, then looking askance at my outfit before handing over a Rotterdam Shopping Guide, her verdict was unanimous, with herself.

No, these are hard to find. You will not find one of these in the Netherlands.

Pretty definite there. I applauded her certainty but cursed her confidence.

The next best thing would be a micro USB charger. Listen, if you think this is dull, try living it – this was supposed to be an odyssey and I'm buying mobile phone accessories at 9am.

With shops closed until 10am, it was time to browse the windows in the shopping centre and camp out like an 11-year-old waiting for boyband tickets to go on sale.

Suddenly, through the grill of a phone shop, there it was – my two-pronged saviour. In an hour it would be mine. The plan was to grab a coffee, consult the Interrail map and work out where I was heading next with pen and paper. Unfortunately the only place open with a sightline of the store was those golden arches.

The sacrifice of principles was painful but armed with an acceptable coffee that needed to last an hour, I sat on a high stool facing out and began the stakeout, avoiding any disapproving looks from the highly motivated counter staff who had plastic eggs to push. Only half an hour later I spotted my knight with shiny charger rolling up the grill.

Coffee abandoned, he had barely made it back behind the counter when my card was in the machine. Weena was a blur as I rushed to sink the little beauty into the socket and resurrect the phone.

With an hour until check-out and little else to do until there was a decent percentage of juice, the kitchen was calling. The fear was fish eye broth and vodka but the table welcomed me with the usual spread of breads, fruit, spreads, and a boiled egg. She reached into the fridge and brought out a plate of sausage.

No sausage, thank you.

You no want sausage?

No, thank you.

Why you no want sausage?

I just don't eat much meat… if that's OK?

Shrug. *Here is yoghurt. I will be in office.*

Aside from that sparkling exchange, it transpired that her home was Ukraine but she had been in Rotterdam for many years. She was keen to discuss the Scottish independence referendum of 2014 too. That's how, on a sunny Rotterdam morning, I found myself explaining the 1707 Union of the Crowns to a Ukrainian landlady.

By the time check-out time came, I had enough power to book a room in Breda. As well as having had a recommendation from a colleague many years before, it was only 30 minutes away, leaving the full day for Rotterdam.

With the backpack confined to yet another locker, there was a 10 kilometre roaming route on the tourist map to follow, one which seemed to tick some of my boxes and throw in a few extras. The new walking shoes were great but still not broken in completely. Still, it was nothing that couldn't be rectified by the liberal application of blister cushions. This was also the hottest day so far, which meant breaking out the Factor 50. Despite the heat heading north of 30 degrees and being aware that there was some significant chafing around the heels, it was a glorious day.

Rotterdam was annihilated during the Second World War. With little surviving, it decided not to rebuild the medieval city, but start again. Rotterdam decided it could be anything.

The incredible market hall, surely a gift from the aliens, with its food markets below and apartments above, was the next dream home. This time it would be an ultra-modern bachelorette pad at the top of the horseshoe-shaped building, where I could buy my clean eating, organic goodies for the week downstairs, waving to the stallholders as I go, then head out on my bicycle looking effortlessly stylish with two Jack Russells trotting alongside. That's the benefit of being without a base – imagining a new life anywhere isn't being disloyal to home.

Buying bottled water for the next part of the day pulled me out of that fantasy. I could see the checkout operator's mouth moving, but even the context didn't help to compute. There was instant regret that I hadn't had more time to plan and get a few stock phrases in place. However, I tried not to beat myself up for not being able to understand the Dutch for *Do you have a loyalty card?*

As the temperature rose, more locals came to sunbathe along the Nieuwe Maas, with clothing discarded and much smooching. For them. I headed across the Erasmus Bridge, my destination being the far end of the cruise terminal and a slice of Rotterdam's more glamorous past. The Hotel New York is the former headquarters of the Holland America Line. A building that screams Gatsby and flappers and cocktails, the outdoor café was the end of this line and the place to stop for a local brew.

In such sociable surroundings it becomes clear pretty quickly that you're sitting alone – that sounds better than drinking alone. Three particularly well-dressed ladies arrived walking two long-haired Dachshunds who were panting loudly enough to hear over the gentle beer-infused burble. My beer was almost done and with no food since breakfast I wouldn't have another, but until those little dogs had a bowl of water I couldn't move on. They found shade under the table, but I wanted to see a sign that the ladies would ask for water bowls along with their continental cocktails. I nursed my dregs until their salads arrived, along with water. The dogs lapped furiously and their tails wagged to match. I asked for the bill.

The old port area used to be a place where sailors could roll off the boats and straight into the red light district but now it's lined with delis, designer shops, and galleries. The sun was still fierce in the late afternoon, and the walk back over bridge and on to the station took me through the dock area where the contents of shipping containers are no longer cargo, but art.

Heading into the Museumpark, I was stopped in my tracks by the ghostly sound of Connie Francis singing *Who's Sorry Now?* A couple were embracing and swaying slowly to the music, completely lost in the moment – and one another. They really were dancing like no-one was watching. When the music stopped, they parted slightly, kissed lightly, laughed, and walked away.

Only then did I notice the source of the music, a Public Jukebox loaded with songs of all genres and languages and completely free to listen. I chose one at random and sat on the steps in front. I had no idea what the song was but it was a wistful farewell to the city.

The half-hour journey to Breda was a welcome break for my feet. The hotel I had booked looked pretty spectacular for the price. Of course, location hadn't come into the decision. It wasn't in the old town, I knew that, but heading out on a long straight road from the station, I wondered whether another self-imposed ban, this time on taking taxis, should end.

Pausing for a moment to slug water and rearrange blister plasters, a kindly looking couple stopped and asked if they could help. This was the right road, it seemed. It was another 450m until a set of traffic lights, then the hotel was 600m after that. Got to love that precision.

The exterior of Hotel Scheepshuys was promising and I was keen to see if the inside matched. If I get could get in. The owner, who lives off-site, had asked about my arrival time. I was pretty spot on saying 7pm and arriving at 7.15, but she hadn't arrived. A young man unloading his car let me into the foyer and suggested that I buzz an intercom. The owner answered and said she would be there in seven minutes. Again, precise.

It was exquisite inside – clearly a former home with beautiful wood panels and stained glass over the wide staircase.

The tour included my upgraded room and a dream kitchen (I was off again… just think Jack Russells and being effortlessly stylish) with a fridge that included free water, soft drinks, and beer. Perhaps I reacted too enthusiastically, being reminded gently that it was for the whole house.

There was the small issue of food. With no restaurants around, the best I could do was get to a shop and cook for myself. It was 7.40pm and the shop shut at 8pm, so it was time to hobble as fast as my newly sprung blisters would let me down Ignatiusstraat and into a shopping area that, surprisingly, would have worked pretty well as the backdrop to any Joy Division video. Back at the Scheepshuys with food in the fridge, enjoying a free beer in the garden before dinner was the way to decompress while the phone was charging to a lovely 100%, which would allow me to find out more about where the hell I was.

The only other person there was the same young man, who I now know was Ferdinand. There were a few polite nods, and soon the dance of *shall*

I come over to you or you to me? was over and we sat clinking our complimentary Amstels. As it turned out, it was his stag night. *I* was his stag night really. His wedding was the next day, but as he lived with his fiancée they decided he would stay away the night before – even though he lived only a few houses away from this hotel.

The evening sun was glorious and the garden was tranquil but after an hour I could see the tell-tale sign of bites to my arm. Another hour on and a fever had settled. The food stayed in the fridge and I raided the water before heading to bed. The next morning it was obvious that I wouldn't be travelling anywhere that day. As the breakfast spread was given a wide berth I booked another night, hoping that I would feel well enough to explore at least the old part of town at some point.

That afternoon, even Breda's charms were lost on me. The bites had swollen, I had lobster pink sunburn from Rotterdam, and the ankle chafing had taken its toll. The only saving grace was an elegant hotel with cool cotton sheets in a comfortable bed. The best plan was to recover for the next day, however long it took to shuffle back there. For some reason catching a taxi still didn't occur to me.

The next stop would be Utrecht. Again it was only an hour away, so health permitting there could be another quick stop before, but that would be decided when I stood up in the morning.

The standing up was successful despite a fitful night's sleep due to whatever the bugs had injected into my system. The improvement was promising enough to make a brief stopover at Gouda. It was on the way and it was all about cheese. The temperatures were still mid to high 20s, which keeps it officially comfortable. Maybe not for carrying a backpack, however. With no luggage lockers at the station, this would be the first experience of carrying it in the heat for a few hours.

There is more to Gouda than cheese, but they do tend to keep the cheese front, centre, and above with chunky spaceships of orange goodness dangling on wires strung high across the smaller shopping streets. From the cheese museum at tourist information to the market opposite selling, well mostly cheese really, Gouda knows its unique selling point.

For the lactose intolerant it's a still an attractive town with sleepy canals. Along the canal sides, directly outside the tidy houses, the number of Stolpersteine was remarkable. These are brass plaques on cobblestones outside the last-known addresses of those who fell victim to the Nazi slaughter. The work of artist Gunter Demnig, it wasn't the first location in which I had spotted these, but the number for such a relatively small town was overwhelming. Some homes will have more than one plaque, where several members or even entire families were lost. They are now found throughout Europe and beyond, as Demnig raises sponsorship to honour as many Jews and people from all groups who were persecuted or murdered under that regime. That type of distraction helps to forget about the small weight you're carrying.

Travel, in the younger sort, is a part of education;
in the elder, a part of experience.

Francis Bacon

ARRIVING IN UTRECHT was something of an anti-climax after the instant delights of Gouda. Passengers are scattered from the platforms straight into the Hoog Catharijne shopping centre, apparently the largest mall in the Netherlands, if such a thing can be a boast.

Thankfully it was a brief blip. Heading further into town, it was a cheerful Saturday evening with crowds gathering on the streets, along the canals, and in the pavement cafés. More cheerful still was the fact that I found my bed for the next two nights easily.

This was the first full-on hostel experience, sharing a dormitory with three other people. While recognising that for most backpackers this is the norm, I was so far outside my comfort zone that I couldn't see its circumference. Although there was no splurging on accommodation, I was fortunate enough to take the next small step to hostel private rooms or small hotels. The glowing reviews for this hostel encouraged me to push the personal boundaries.

The stairs to reception were the first challenge – there had been no instructions to bring climbing gear so the only way to prevent a tumble backwards was to hold on to the stairs in front, much like a giant turtle scaling the side of a building.

The room was up another flight, this time with a sharp turn, which must have trapped those with backpacks bigger than mine. I was clearly struggling and the receptionist offered some help, but all I could hear was *Don't you dare die on us old woman.*

A top bunk had been assigned, accessed by a metal ladder which shoogled at the slightest touch. My last experience of bunk beds had been at the age of 15, when my older sister would poke between the spars to annoy me. Highly entertaining for her it seemed.

The room was clean and bright and the fact that others had left open luggage lying around as opposed to using lockers showed a trust in their fellow travellers. Apart from a quick trip to the supermarket for supplies (deposited in the fridge in a plastic box with my name written on it – yeah baby, let's hostel) the remainder of the evening was given over to catching up with notes and thinking ahead a couple of steps. It was a Saturday night in a university town and I was going to have a wee salad and catch up on work. This was never going to be a conventional backpacking trip.

Working in the common area was hopeless. There were too many distractions – even Bilstraat outside the window was worth losing a few dreamy moments to. At least I managed to have a conversation, with a quick check that the denture fixative was doing its work. Omar, a well-travelled Algerian engineer, was staying here while visiting friends he had met on a previous European journey. Jordan, a 21-year-old who had just graduated, was travelling alone for a couple of weeks. She was beautifully honest when asked why she was travelling alone: *I didn't have anyone else to do it with, but why should that stop me?* Good lass.

They had been at the hostel for a day or so and were heading out for a stroll. Even though it was enjoyable to talk with people who weren't checking me in or checking my pass, the thought of heading out with people who were essentially strangers didn't really appeal.

With a few pages of notes done, the common room was invaded by a group of strapping young men who could have easily been a Dutch rowing team. They switched on the common room television to find the Champions League Final between Juventus and Barcelona. They appeared to be enjoying their own shouting competition even more, however, which meant the room was no longer the best environment for reflection.

There was a desk and chair in the dorm but it was covered with the belongings of others and I wasn't hostel-savvy enough to know the etiquette of moving it. The alternative was to head to my top bunk and get an early start the next day. It would also avoid having to hide in the bathroom to change into some form of nightwear.

I was beaten to it. The other top bunk inhabitant was already under the summer weight duvet. I said hello. She looked at me (through me actually) and back to her phone. So, the bathroom it was.

Confession time – nightwear isn't generally my thing, so without official PJs, it was a T-shirt and light leggings. The first rung of the ladder was unnaturally high, and slender metal rungs seemed to target the still tender parts of my feet. Once under the duvet the leggings came off.

I played with my phone for a while, trying to be like the young person opposite, but soon tried to get some sleep. It was uneasy. The presence of other people in the room, the noise from downstairs, the coming and goings of two more roommates – I can sleep through thunderstorms but the strangers unnerved me. The next morning I clambered down after wriggling back into the leggings. The young Japanese girl who had occupied the other top bunk was already in the bathroom, so I waited at the window. Twenty minutes later it was clear she was taking her time, so I gathered my courage and went down to the common shower room. I came back up, dressed, and did a little research on what the day held. It was an hour since I clambered down the ladder and she was still in the bathroom.

I had a quiet 10 minutes in the common room grabbing some breakfast before the lads were back, still without any form of volume control it seemed, so it was time to grab what I needed and leave for the day. It was an early start for a Sunday morning.

My bottom bunkmate had emerged; a tall, glamorous 32-year-old American woman called Coriann, who had been travelling for a couple of months but had been enjoying fairly long stays in each destination. She said her friends had been surprised at the decision to travel alone and they felt she was running away from something. There had been no real reason, she said, not believing in all that travelling for a reason stuff. I kept quiet. An hour or so later I saw her again, this time at a pavement café, sipping coffee and looking as if she had wafted down from her apartment upstairs rather than a four-bed dorm with a few hours of sleep.

The receptionist at the hotel handed over a city map. Clearly not looking for a job with the local tourist office, she said that Utrecht didn't have any main sights but it was a good place to wander. Recalling the disappointment in so many destinations that exaggerated the charms of a museum of broken pottery, I appreciated this honesty. I also liked that it was so early all cyclists were still in their effortlessly stylish apartments, eating healthy breakfasts and preparing for a day of terrorising pedestrians.

That first Sunday came with church bells that did more than add ambience. As they pealed a steady stream of people entered the churches. I know that's the point but it felt slightly creepy. A morning market around Domplein attracted those who found their spiritual home among the stalls and giant rabbits. The rabbits appeared across the city, in a variety of guises. These were all Miffy, or Nintje as she's known here. The simply drawn rabbit created by Utrecht artist Dick Bruin 60 years before was being celebrated by artists using Miffy's blank canvas to give the beloved bunny any personality they desired – the Ninja Nintje was particularly interesting.

It seemed that bicycles were uppermost in the city's collective mind, however. The Tour de France was due to begin here in a few weeks and there were many, many, many reminders. Down at the old canal, with Winkel van Sinkel, a cultural and culinary destination opposite, I tried to get the best possible shot of its highly amusing name. In doing so, I backed into a parked bicycle. It was always going to happen.

This was parked alongside many others, however, and as I saw it lean, in my head an unceasing line of bicycles toppled like dominoes. The next few seconds stretched into an eternity. The collapse stayed at one, thank goodness, but instead of trying to stand it up, I walked away. There were enough eyes on me without trying to pick it up and risking a scenario worthy of Norman Wisdom, where my head would end up through one set of spokes and a leg through another.

Skulking away from the canal area, there was live music in a park with families picnicking and people throwing dogs for balls. Jack Russell Terriers or some slight variation were everywhere. I sat on a bench having grabbed a coffee from a stall and listened to a competent duo on the bandstand. It had been a long walking day and although I didn't have a problem with eating alone, there hadn't been many temptations to sit down and enjoy something local so far. It was evening, the phone charge was fading and decisions still had to be made about the next few days, so it was back to the hostel common room.

Tonight it resounded to the merriment of drum and bass. No sooner had I taken a seat with some bread, cheese, and a beer, a young man in a canary yellow tracksuit and beer goggles approached with what he reckoned were his best chat-up lines. This wasn't Geena Davis and Brad Pitt in *Thelma and Louise*. This was horrific. He grasped a can of lager with all his might and opened with the spectacular.

You like cheese? I like cheese too baby.

I do like cheese, but the edible sort. I can even stomach the musical variety. After politely declining invitations to join him, he shrugged while swaying and pointing at nothing in particular.

You need sausage with your cheese…

I decided to take that as a culinary tip rather than as a saucy euphemism and left the room.

A new girl had joined the dorm, an Italian who was sitting at the desk, so it was from the discomfort of the top bunk that the decision was made to linger in the Netherlands a while.

Monday morning found the Japanese girl in the bathroom, while down-stairs was also occupied. I left unshowered and unfed and feeling like a true backpacker.

Heading to the train station involved finding the shopping centre again, but drawing near there was the distraction of a giant teapot on the flyover. A few steps ahead was a man who looked like a commuter, so why not follow? All these doors would get me into the centre somehow, then on into the station. He sprinted up a flight of stairs. With the pack my ascent was more of a trudge – and he was lost to me.

Trying several side doors that led to nothing I needed, one door led to an open lift, which at least offered some escape. Pressing 0 did nothing. Jabbing at buttons in a random fashion did nothing. When the lift door opened again, an elderly lady looked at me with some horror and it's hardly surprising. There was a red-faced woman swearing in a totally incomprehensible language (in this case Dundonian) in the service elevator of her workplace. Thank goodness the tooth stayed in.

As a shared experience this would have been hilarious; alone it was humiliating. Having finally found the correct way into the centre, which truly is the place for any remake of George Romero's *Day of the Dead*, the next destination was Haarlem, just 50 minutes away. On board, the announcements were clearly about Haarlem; this was clear by the liberal use of the word Haarlem. A girl sitting opposite obviously saw the gormless expression and explained that trains wouldn't be stopping there today, with a bus running from Amsterdam.

In the vast Amsterdam central station and aware that I couldn't even make my way into a shopping centre that morning, getting to the information centre was crucial. Without some guidance I could end up back in Brussels. On arrival at the desk, however, a laidback assistant waved lazily and told me that the problem was over, everything had been sorted 27 minutes ago. Again precise.

Catching the next train to Haarlem was my first journey with no seat, but it was 18 minutes at most. I was catching the precision. There was no point in unloading the pack and folding the straps away, but conscious of knocking a child on to the tracks with any sudden movement, I squished as close to the wall of the train as possible.

Mine was still the smallest pack I had seen so far. The glamorous American had examined it in detail, thinking that for three months of travelling there had to be a door that opened, Narnia-like, into another pack. The wardrobe was limited certainly, and the laundry section was beginning to overtake the clean clothing, but apart from a couple of stupid decisions made in London, everything I needed was there.

Despite the brief layover in Amsterdam, I had arrived in Haarlem well before the agreed check-in time. There was no worry about getting lost – it wasn't a metropolis that would swallow me into its belly – oooooh, look there's a windmill.

The next two nights were to be spent on a canal boat, so heading away from water wasn't the best idea. From the picture on the booking app, it wasn't clear what the boat looked like but after a respectable amount of time (progress was being made) there it was, with a smiley blonde captain providing a hearty welcome aboard.

Having to go down rather than up, a beer crate provide the extra step into the boat. It didn't look particularly secure though, so taking the pack off first was paramount to preventing a comedy tumble into the canal.

The captain looked like a Dutch Olympic fencing champion and was charming if not thorough in her welcome. Here's the code for the outside, here's your cabin key, here are some towels, and breakfast is at 8.30am, see ya... and she bounced off. I was alone on a canal boat in Haarlem.

It was a tiny cabin with bunk beds, a sink, and a wardrobe. Along the corridor were shared toilets and shower rooms, but the lounge area made up for the basic facilities down below. For a while this was my new dream home – the Jack Russells had tiny lifejackets and the bicycle was tied up outside.

For a while... Too soon, there was a middle-aged man trying to steady himself on the beer crate and poking at the keypad. Presuming he was a guest it was only fair to let him in. At first there was no convincing him that I wasn't the captain, despite the fact that I wasn't Dutch and she had left fulsome instructions, his keys, and a note to say he could pay at breakfast. There were French mutterings (he was French) before he headed off into Haarlem to find something 'natural' to smoke in his electronic cigarette.

The whole day was ahead, and without recourse to shopping or visiting every museum, Haarlem can be explored in a day. It's no wonder so many people who work in Amsterdam choose to call this home. There is enough shopping (for me anyway) and mellow residential areas with quiet cafés and bars. There was nothing particularly remarkable but that's what made it so attractive – nothing had to be ticked off a list. I could just *be* in Haarlem, wandering and daydreaming and knowing that wherever I turned, the streets would be charming and the houses totally dinky. Perhaps two nights here had been hasty, however. As close as it was, I didn't want to go to Amsterdam the next day. I had been there before and the plan was to avoid major capitals where possible. Looking at alternative day trip destinations, The Hague was only 40 minutes away.

The evening passed in the comfort of the lounge, watching the canal traffic and many rowers. The Frenchman reappeared and promptly disappeared below, and a young dark-haired man who was apparently another guest materialised from nowhere. He left and returned half a dozen times that evening, keeping his hands in his pockets at all times, even when negotiating the crate.

There was no sign of him at breakfast – perhaps no-one else knew he was there. The captain was definitely there, bopping around to a music radio station that had taken me 20 minutes to switch off the day before, and setting out the cereals, cheese… the usual.

The pass came into its own for decisions like this. A quick check of the app to confirm that no further reservations were required and it was time to jump on a train.

It was a grey day in The Hague. It's a destination that really only passes our lips when we suggest who should be there being tried for war crimes. There were identikit shopping streets and some small squares, but this day visit was taken up with the pursuit of justice – and that's not too shabby. Taking the long walk up to the International Criminal Tribunal for the Former Yugoslavia and down a boulevard where multi-coloured flags added some life to the grey skies and concrete backdrops, the finishing point was The Peace Palace, still a working building as the International Court of Justice, so off limits for the full visit that day.

The concourse outside on Carnegieplein, named for Scottish philanthropist Andrew Carnegie who financed the building, is paved with the word peace in every language, as well as colourful mosaics depicting peace doves and nations reaching out to one another. A moment of contemplation was interrupted by a busload of noisy tourists on a quick photo stop, but once they had their five minutes and a box ticked, peace was restored. It's a tidy city though and with more time I might have experienced more of what was covered in a slick introductory film shown in the sparkling, modern town hall.

Back in Haarlem on the boat, a young couple had joined the crew, drinking with some authority and planning to catch a train to Amsterdam to *pardeeeeeeee*. Their word, not mine.

The dark-haired man arrived again and disappeared below, before the Frenchman appeared, stuck his head above deck meerkat-style, and disappeared below again. What was down there? Did they have palatial suites?

Still, the quiet allowed me time to think about where was next. After eight days it was time to experience something different from market squares and canals. Looking at the map, the islands off the northern tip of the Netherlands were intriguing, particularly as I hadn't realised there were islands there. I would always recommend that people visiting Scotland should go to an island, so maybe I could follow my own advice here.

Early the next morning, having booked three nights in a hotel, I was hurrying to head off to the island of Texel. There was another reason for the hasty exit.

Feeling alone on the boat most of the time, I had been rather cavalier with the lock on the bathroom door. That morning, the Frenchman had yanked the door open and I swear exclaimed *Zut alors*! I'm not sure what was more embarrassing – being caught with my pants down or the fact that I was using my phone at the time – still, at least it prevented full foof exposure.

We were excessively polite to one another as I left to catch the train to Den Helder and connect with the ferry to an island that, 24 hours previously, I didn't even know existed. The journey needed a change of pace and I hoped this would be the answer. From the Art Nouveau beauty of Haarlem station we were soon sitting for a suspiciously long time at a station in the middle of the Dutch countryside.

The reaction around me to an announcement was enough to realise that the news wasn't good. The train wouldn't be heading to Alkmaar, the connection station. After being turfed out on to the platform, we trundled over to the bus station to reach Alkmaar. One bus filled up and it was clear that I was in a position to be on the third or fourth. The buses were an hour apart.

Completely bemused and resigned to getting to Texel late or if at all that day, when a train arrived I did what anyone in my position would. I followed a group who looked like they knew what they were doing. In this case it paid off and we were heading back to Amsterdam Sloterdijk where there was a connection to Den Helder.

For whatever we lose (like a you or a me),
It's always ourselves we find in the sea.
e.e. cummings

THERE WERE ADDITIONAL delays, but of the mundane kind. At least by late afternoon I had reached Den Helder and was buying a ferry ticket to Texel. From the train to a bus to walking on to the ferry on a glorious June day, the prospect of going over water to the unknown had elevated my excitement about this journey.

There's nothing like wind whipping hair around the face, as long as a hat is held firmly in your hand. My cream sunhat hadn't had many outings yet, but it felt like something of a mascot. Bought almost 20 years ago, it had travelled from Canada to Australia to India and more. It had also survived the rigours of music festivals, as a protection from rain as well as sun. It wouldn't have survived this blowy 20-minute ferry crossing.

From the ferry it was easy to catch the Texel Hopper, a small blue bus that acted as something of a taxi service, taking islanders as close to their front doors as possible. Not just islanders, but visitors too. My hotel was in De Cocksdorp at the north end of the island, so I was the last passenger to leave. Instead of dropping me at the designated stop, he inched along Kirk-straat and stopped at the door of the Hotel het Anker van Texel. For once, the accommodation was easy to find.

I did doubt that this was the correct hotel, however. If it had been lifted and placed on a Scottish island it would have been beyond my budget. The owners, Margreet and Bas, had moved from Groningen only a couple of months before and had already created a comfortable, stylish and affordable boutique hotel.

For the next couple of days this would be the perfect place to relax, walk, take stock, and have a think about how the journey should progress. Aware that I had spent a lot of time in the Netherlands, I considered whether the three months could be extended further. Then I stopped thinking so much and lived in the moment.

At the north end of Kirkstraat were the beaches of the Wadden Sea, but before that was the dike, where Texel sheep grazed and watched those below with a superiority that comes from knowing how important their wool is to the island economy.

It didn't take long to wander around De Cocksdorp. Dinner was eaten at a wooden table near a Kirkstaat stall selling fresh fish and the best chunky frites on the planet (sorry Belgium) accompanied by a bottle of Texels, a local red ale. I had a sense of deep contentment that felt unfamiliar but satisfying.

The room was small and comfortable, and the fact that I had two full days here meant that some overdue laundry could be done that night and hung on the travel washing line.

Over a breakfast of goodies including homemade bread and jam from local strawberries, homemade yoghurt and Texel sheep cheese, Margreet was keen to introduce her guests to one another. I had breakfast with the dynamic Jakob from Maastricht. A retired chemist and research scientist, he was here to walk and on that day was heading to Vlieland. At 70, he had the stance and gait of a man 30 years younger and in good shape. He was travelling solo, having lost his wife in an accident 20 years before, and September would see him in South America, travelling through the continent for seven months – inspirational. We said our goodbyes and he strapped on his backpack, steadied his poles and headed out to walk the half hour to the ferry.

Consulting a map, well it seems that's what they're for, it showed that walking along the dike through the sheep would take me to the beach. I was at the gate and preparing to walk among the sheep of Texel. I had checked with Margreet that this was allowed and was happy to hear: *Yes, you can walk among them, they are not dangerous*. Never the most physically dextrous, the simplest gate could prove a problem to me – and it did. The sheep regarded this new presence with some interest, but less so when I finally made it through to their patch. The walking shoes were never more welcome. Walking among the sheep of Texel also meant walking among their doings.

The views from the dike to the left were over De Cocksdorp and the Roggesloot nature reserve, while to the right I could see an expanse of white beach and out to sea. What a start to the day. Cloudless blue skies and sheep that weren't dangerous.

Approaching the next gate, the way was blocked by a generously fleeced mama sheep and her little one. There was no way mama was moving, however, and I feared that opening the gate might lead to the great Texel stampede of 2015. So it was time to clamber, the sheep regarding this with all the respect it deserved.

It was abandoned at the first wobble. Toppling into sheep faeces, breaking a leg, and being airlifted off the island, only to be told my travel insurance didn't cover acts of extreme daftness, didn't appeal. I didn't disclose the fact that I'm hopeless at anything physical.

Time to think came with a seat on a small wooden sticky-out ledge – you can tell I'm a country girl. After a minute or two the youngster sidled over, gave me a quick sniff and frolicked off – followed by mama – allowing me to escape. The further along the dike I walked, the more the beach opened up. The blue sky met the sea with a base level of dazzling white sands. So dazzling that the decision to do without contact lenses and wear glasses through the trip felt like another bad one, particularly with no prescription sunglasses. The light was so bright that the sand was blinding. Past the line of people waiting to board the boat to Vlieland, the beach was deserted and the ice-cream coloured beach huts were locked up.

The sand was so soft that it had to be done. The shoes came off and the sand trickled through my toes. It felt OK. Not particularly pleasant but another small victory in the self-confidence crusade. More than warm, this sand was toasty and almost too hot to bear. And in the distance was a familiar figure. Small, tan and white in colour, and digging in the sand as if Australia was offering free chicken for life. There was also the particularly insistent bark that demanded a ball be thrown again immediately. It cut through the sound of the sea and was clearly the same in any language.

As I came closer and began something of a stealth stalk, it was Kali, my Jack Russell Terrier. Of course it wasn't, she had died the previous July, but this was Kali reincarnated. I hovered closely enough for the couple to notice how enchanted I was with their four-legged chum and I hoped for an invitation to pat a small head and say hello. We spoke briefly. They were on holiday from Eindhoven and little Dinus (he) was 13 years old, the age that Kali reached. He was Kali's male twin, except that he brought the ball back. Like everyone else I had met here, he was remarkably fit and sprightly for his age. I wouldn't have been surprised if he had run up the boardwalk and headed off on his own bicycle.

Before the situation became too weird, I left them paddling in the shallows and headed off again, glancing back from time to time until Dinus became a tiny speck on the blinding horizon. I headed for the dunes and wept for Kali. I had been inconsolable and frankly slightly unhinged when another

47

Jack Russell, Chili, had died four years before Kali, so I had tried to act in what I considered a more dignified way after losing her. If I was going to have my first major howl since she died, I couldn't have chosen a more beautiful place to do it. Eyes dried, I took a couple of slugs of water to rehydrate and carried on.

I had been heading to the lighthouse, situated at the point, with the intention to head around the coast and walk back inland towards the village. Kite flyers and more dog walkers added spots of colour to the white sands. Settling in the dunes I could hear some commotion nearby. Tanned, toned, and with two cherubic children, it was a family surely planted by the Texel Tourist Board.

He was obviously an architect, with his own ecologically sound practice, while she was an academic of scientific repute in some top European seat of learning. They were here for a few days before the parents went off for the annual together time – building green homes and schools in Africa. The child prodigies would be off to the HufHaus of one set of grandparents (the others would be invited because, of course, they all got on famously). The silver foxes and vixens would show the grandchildren how to bake, be mindful, and probably play the bloody cello in the space of a week.

It's amazing what open spaces, clear skies, and time to think can do to the imagination.

The upshot was that they had everything. I had nothing of course. With a failed marriage (not bothered) and a failed long-term relationship (still bothered) behind me, and a body that couldn't conceive, conventional family life had never happened. At 48 and following a hysterectomy it never would – now it was time to embrace that rather than accept it. If only for a second one child had a tantrum, spat out the homemade kale crisps and demanded some chicken nuggets. It would have punctured the fantasy that anyone, anywhere lives a perfect life. All this torture and self-pity and it wasn't even noon. With no-one to make you snap out of it, it's easier to wallow. However, with no-one to help you get out of it, it feels so much better when you do.

Whether it was the heat, the sun, or the mood, I didn't feel like eating at the beach café, but it was a welcome oasis to replenish water supplies for the afternoon's walking. Heading back cross-country through strange scrub, it was clear how much the temperature had taken out of me that day. Back in De Cocksdorp and stopping off at the small supermarket, my cash reserves were low but there was an ATM, which it transpired didn't take my kind of card. Neither did the checkout, so buying that night's dinner left me with only a few emergency Euros.

I wouldn't need much, however. The plan for the next day was to see the south of the island, including the main village of Den Burg. The map showed that it could be reached on foot by taking a coastal path and heading inland. Already feeling fitter than the day I left Dundee, the prospect of walking the 16km from De Cocksdorp to Oudeschilde then another 4km into Den Burg didn't seem too taxing. In fact, walking was becoming one of the best parts of the journey. The lucky hat, Factor 50 sun protection, and plenty of water would keep me safe. The walking shoes were broken in and were free of the sand they gathered the day before.

Breakfast was busier that morning, mostly with couples, but one woman came in alone and sat at a corner table. Apart from hotel staff, ticket inspectors, and yesterday's chat with Jakob, Margreet, and Bas it had been a while since I had a conversation of more than a few words, so when she invited me to join her, it seemed like a good idea.

It was. Helma was here for a short break from her home in Amsterdam, where she is second bassoonist with the city's Concertgebouw Orchestra. Her boyfriend is also an orchestra member and they live together, so they think it's healthy to spend a few days apart from time to time. It is.

She was also heading south but had a car and offered me a lift. It would take a few kilometres from the walk, but I could make that up by going at least part of the way back on foot. It also gave me the chance to see another village and get to know Helma a little better.

Arriving in Oosterend, we didn't have the familiarity to explore together yet, so we parted ways and agreed to meet up for a drink later. For the next 10 minutes there was the faintly embarrassing experience of crossing paths several times, with smiles and nods and *oh no, not again* eye rolls.

She drove off and I spent a little more time in the glorious village, remembering to stock up on water. I had just enough funds to do that before heading out of the village to find Lancasterdijk, the path that would take me down the east coast and straight into Oudeschilde.

It will come as no surprise that I somehow lost the path and joined further up the dike at the village of Oost, adding 2km to the walk. The long, straight path was flanked on one side by the sea, and on the other by the dike housing some familiar faces. They weren't the same sheep of course, but were clearly related.

Even with the preparation, the walk became torturous quite quickly. The temperature soared and the path was more suited to cycling. Strange glances from well-toned individuals on racing bikes and elderly couples on tring tring bikes with panier baskets made me feel like an alien from some distant civilisation that hadn't quite caught up with the wheel. Even the sheep looked on in disdain, their baas echoing along the dike: *you're never going to believe what's coming – walking. I know. Walking!*

The route never changed. The sea and sky were blue, the sheep were bemused and the road was relentless. The only blessing was the fact that it was flat. In less than 30 degree heat it might have been bearable, but the lack of shade and trying to ration water meant that for too long a stretch I was sipping from a bottle containing water that was hot enough to comfortably accommodate a teabag.

The map indicated a windmill at Oudeschilde. For who knows how long I stared into the distance praying for the arms of a windmill to puncture the nothingness of the skyline.

When it came into sight, I took the final wincing gulp of the warm water and looked forward to replenishing my supplies. A busy tourist harbour like this, with bonny fish restaurants and ice-cream and beer and everything, they would take my cards. Wouldn't they?

Trying not to get teary or angry or cursing everyone in Oudeschilde, the next 4km walk to Den Burg without water at least had some distractions. The Texels Brewery wasn't the best, however, with hallucinations of a frosted bottle in my hand. When Den Burg appeared I felt like Dorothy reaching Oz. The aim was to find a bank and then the darkest, coolest bar possible. Thankfully both were on the first street. The barmaid was perceptive and immediately poured a pint of cold water before serving me beer. Then another.

Then a sweet, sweet Texels with free cheese and salty snacks. It was a great bar with friendly punters, my favourite music including Hall & Oates and, man oh man, some ELO! Then a dog arrived. I could so easily have kept the Texels coming, sang along to AOR too loudly and been crap at pool. In reality, I would have fallen off the stool with no charge on the phone, crying at my stupidity.

Den Burg was soothing in the early evening light, with tasteful souvenir shops and narrow alleyways busy with locals and visitors, some of whom were even on foot.

I called the Texel Hopper and the driver told me where to meet it in Den Burg. There would be no more walking that day – I had started at 11am and hadn't stopped until after 5pm. Back on the cool cotton sheets of the bed in De Cocksdorp, any notion of meeting anyone for a drink disappeared and my tootsies were set free. Maybe after a nap. A nap became a full night's sleep.

Margreet and Bas had made their previous home of Groningen sound pretty enchanting, so I would spend one more night in the Netherlands instead of heading straight to Germany. The morning was grey and drizzly and Helma was already at breakfast. It seemed no apology was necessary. She had also fallen asleep and was about to apologise to me. Again she offered me a lift to the south of the island, this time right to Den Hoorn where I would catch the ferry.

Checking out was cheery, but the atmosphere changed when the curse of Visa Debit struck again. The hotel didn't take it. I had some cash, withdrawn in Den Burg, but trying not to carry too much I couldn't cover the three nights. On the hotel laptop, my online banking wouldn't allow a transfer to an account outside of the UK. So, left with no way to pay, the wonderful Helma stepped in. We would drive to Den Burg where I could repay her. I felt dreadful but she appeared to think it was an amusing adventure.

It was Saturday in Den Burg and busy. The streets were packed and there wasn't a parking space to be had. Helma dropped me off and did laps of a supermarket car park, also full. I tore along the street, found an ATM, and with a decent stock of precious Euros in my hand ran back along the street. And lost a sandal. Turning back, it was there, in the melee of shoppers.

A few weeks before, a scenario in which I was hunting a sandal in the middle of a village on a Dutch island, while the second bassoonist of the Amsterdam Concertgebouw Orchestra circled the Albert Hejin car park waiting for me, was something beyond hallucinogenic.

Back in the car and fully shod, Helma was so good-natured that I didn't mind laughing when that errant crown fell out in my hand. When she dropped me off at Den Hoorn her slender frame was crushed by my massive, genuine hug.

Back on the mainland, I realised the confusion that missing out a bus journey to the ferry had caused. The passengers had boarded the bus while it was still on the ferry and were now en route to Den Helder train station. As a foot passenger, I was alone at the port and had to get to the station. There were no taxis, but I was assured that it was only 20 minutes away. It was if you walk in the right direction.

Exploring more of Den Helder than was necessary or desirable, the showerproof jacket lived up to its name and couldn't resist the downpour that cascaded in a teeny waterfall from the peak of my cap. Sheltering from the rain for a minute only allowed the cold to seep into my bones, so carrying on was the preferred option.

From the outward journey, there was a memory of a small coffee shop at the station. Thank goodness it wasn't imaginary. Armed with a hot chocolate and apple pie, I boarded the first leg to Groningen soaked but happy to be on my way to yet another destination I hadn't heard of until a couple of days before.

Most of the Dutch journeys were uneventful. Comfortable, clean, and on time. The countryside was only interesting in the way that anything new is, but the distances were short and in this case it was more about the destination than the journey.

Fewer than four hours later, with a connection at Utrecht, I was in my room in Groningen. It had been straightforward to find and was another surprise. At the Het Paleis the rooms are above a brasserie, with each themed by a Dutch artist. Mine was clearly put together by the minimalist as I played hunt the bed before realising it pulled down from the wall. There was a common area with computers, tables, comfy chairs, and a kitchen – and it was totally deserted. In the hope that it might get livelier later, I had a quick stroll and brought dinner back from the supermarket. No-one showed. Not a soul. Another Saturday night and another conversation with a salad – the wild and crazy ride that the folks back home imagined I'd be having.

With a tooth that could escape at any moment, pasty complexion, spectacles that a close friend told me were extremely ageing, no make-up, and clothing more suited to heading to the hills, hitting the bars of Groningen wasn't ever going to happen.

On another Sunday morning in a Dutch university town, after being eaten by the shower curtain and eating a solitary breakfast, Groningen was quieter than Utrecht. In Grote Markt, stages from the previous night's jazz festival were being broken down and the tourist office, clad in multi-coloured tiles, was about to open its doors. It felt more like a place to live than a place to visit. Canal living, impressive university buildings, and incredible Art Nouveau architecture. Along those canals there were beautifully restored camper vans, several independent record shops, and a good selection of bohemian houseboats.

That Sunday afternoon seemed to offer the possibility of social interaction too. There was the distinct sound of live music in the distance – this was more like it. I'd be in my comfort zone there. Easy to rock up to the bar, have a beer and listen to a band, maybe strike up a conversation. *What? Sing? Me? Nooooo. Really? Ah well, if you insist.*

Approaching the bar it was difficult to identify what they were playing; maybe something by a Dutch band? Getting closer it became clear that it was some approximation of *Yellow* by Coldplay. It didn't merit the investment in a beer yet, but give them another chance. It was Grand Funk Railroad's *Some*

Kind Of Wonderful. Recognisable, which was an improvement. Not my ideal set but if they managed to step up to competence, I would stay. A couple of verses in and I hit the pavement. Initially I made some excuses for them performing in a second language, and then realised that you can't drum in Dutch.

There was no doubt that time was slipping and although I had loved every destination, too much time had been spent in the Netherlands. When it came down to it though, there was no fixed itinerary. No rules.

That night I made a last-minute decision and sent a Facebook message.

Family means that no-one
gets left behind or forgotten.

David Ogden Stiers

ALTHOUGH THE MESSAGE had been sent at the eleventh hour, the response was exactly as predicted.

Yes! Please come to stay!

Germany lay ahead. Conscious that I had visited the country often, it wouldn't prove to be much of a challenge. Language wasn't a massive problem either as I could get by with the basics. So the plan was to step off the solo track, but it would be new destinations and the first time I had visited family here.

Sonja is my cousin. A cousin who only came into our lives around 20 years ago, when she was in her 40s. She is my late Uncle Peter's daughter, born to his German girlfriend who he met when he was serving with the King's Own Borderers and stationed in Celle, north of Hannover.

Like many German children born out of wedlock at that time, Sonja was taken to an orphanage and subsequently adopted by a family in the village of Eschede near Celle, where she still lives and recently retired from her job as an art teacher in the village school. It was only as an adult that Sonja discovered her fraternal roots lay in Scotland, but once she started trying to trace Peter, he had already died at the age of just 46 in 1976. My mother had spoken of his daughter in Germany and the fact that having no access to her had broken his heart, made worse when he had a son with a girlfriend in Dundee, and again he was given no access.

Sonja traced her mother to the south coast of England and with her found two step-brothers. The reunion hadn't been a particularly warm one with her mother but she bonded with her siblings. Although she found out that her father had died, she was keen to meet her Scottish family. It took until 1993 to get some traction when she located my mother, the last remaining sibling of the four Rafferty children. And, of course, another step-brother.

When she visited Dundee for the first time she was able to tell my mother so much about her brother and his time in the Army. Her research was thorough and incredibly detailed but she was missing the human connection – those who knew him. That was the first of many visits – she organised several teacher swap programmes to spend more time in Scotland. I had been living in Glasgow for much of the time when she visited regularly, trying to work my way out of an unsuitable marriage, so we didn't meet often enough during her time in Dundee. No-one had visited her in Germany, however, and I felt a pang of guilt each time I was in the country and hadn't made the effort to reach Eschede. This was the time.

From Groningen the train passed through Bremen. It was a city I hadn't visited, so with the backpack in another locker I had a few hours to take in the remarkable old town. The day was about Eschede, however, reached from the Hannover to Hamburg line. Forty minutes later than expected, I left the train on a perfect summer's evening, made even lovelier by the sight of Sonja running up the platform. Her daughter Ulrike and granddaughter Janna were also there, with Sonja's husband Mekki preparing Abendessen at home.

The seatbelts had barely been fastened before we arrived at the house where Sonja had grown up. She had studied textile design and lived in various locations in Germany but came back to the house in Eschede, working not only as an art teacher, but also as a court artist for the main newspaper in Celle. Mekki is her second husband and had been a cook in the old East when he arrived from his home in Iraq around 50 years ago. He speaks little English but my limited German meant that we had some common linguistic ground, but the real desire to communicate was the key.

In an arrangement that many other couples would love to follow, Mekki stayed at home to look after their two sons when Sonja, as the larger earner, went to work. Mekki still cooks every meal, wonderfully, and Sonja can't let go of her work completely, taking me to school to meet the pupils in a class she takes on a freelance basis.

I was keen to see Celle. It's another German gem – atmospheric and charming, but it would be easy to miss on the better-known tourist trails. As we drove into town Sonja pointed out the British barracks where my uncle had lived. Walking though Celle, even though I was only 10 when he died, I could picture him and his friends heading to the bars to meet local girls. How many had children ended up in Sonja's position?

As we sat in the vestibule of the house in Eschede, she nodded to the front door and said that Peter had been there. When she was around five years old he found out where Sonja had been taken. He arrived at the house and asked to spend time with his daughter, perhaps even take her back to Scotland. The answer was a firm no.

She was told this by her parents who said she was playing in the front garden at the time. Unfortunately she has no recollection of it happening. He had to turn and walk away, with his daughter in full sight. She knew he had come for her. Maybe we only truly appreciate family when you have to fight for it.

The couple of days I spent with Sonja and Mekki were over too quickly. The family dinners, the visits to Lidl, cosying on the sofa and pretending that I understood much more of what was being said on German TV than I did, and looking at Sonja's extensive family research that is also my family research and stretches back to 18th century Ireland.

Sonja and Mekki waved me off at Eschede, always making sure I didn't stand too close to the edge of the platform as the high-speed ICE trains came through – that's the love of family.

I might have been born in Liverpool,
but I grew up in Hamburg.

John Lennon

IT WAS TIME to head north to Scandinavia, but with a short stop in Hamburg to plan the next steps. Hamburg wasn't entirely new to me as I had been on a press trip to the city. To the outside observer press trips are free holidays. Of course the free part is true. There is another name for them, however – familiarisation trips, which is perhaps closer to reality. Journalists are taken off in groups to become familiar with the location, but also with the various organisations that fund the trip. There are small windows of free time, but they tend to be based around an itinerary of what they want you to see, who they want you to meet, what they want you to eat and drink, and where these trips want you to stay. That's fine – it's what you sign up for.

Depending on the mix of journalists in the group, it can be a hoot or hellish. Hamburg was neither. The whole point of the trip was to promote a new direct flight from Newcastle to Hamburg but technical difficulties cancelled the inaugural flight, meaning an extra flight to connect in London. This hacked valuable hours off an already short trip, so once the itinerary was satisfied there had been an hour to look at Hamburg, in the pouring rain. What I did see I liked so this was an opportunity to scrutinise the city at my own pace.

On the train there was a father and two pre-teen children sitting across the aisle. I eavesdropped in a sneaky attempt to test my language listening skills. Not for long though. After a short exchange about where they were staying, dad and the kids took out tablets and sets of headphones, plugged in and tuned out. I couldn't help recalling train journeys as a child, where my dad would sit with me on his knee, pointing out the sheepy mehs and keeping me occupied when the *Beano* and *Dandy* summer specials were exhausted. Two changes of train and Tupperware boxes filled with goodies were all part of the adventure. That's not to say that these children won't look back on a journey with dad with the same fondness, but the experience will be individual rather than shared.

They were still caught up in their games and films when I left the train at Hamburg Hauptbahnhof. This was the first big city of the journey and, to prevent a long and involved wander on arrival, I had looked for the cheapest place near the station.

The receptionist obviously felt that *Fawlty Towers* was a training film on customer service. I hoped that she wouldn't have access to the room, which I was about to turn into a bit of a laundry. Three weeks in, there was a tiny element of homesickness creeping in. Although I had loved my time living with my friend Steve before the journey, it had been several months since I had a bathroom to call my own. Here I had a bathroom with a shelf and surfaces that I could cover with toiletries. Every room became a lounge, bedroom, dining area, and at the moment, an office to look at the finances.

The first tranche of money was disappearing more quickly than expected, even though I had been careful. The final transaction from my recent house sale was delayed more often than nerves could stand, as a portion of the equity would be funding the rest of the trip. If there were significant delays, I'd been heading back with the lucky hat and not too many tales between the covers of my notebook.

Hamburg was out there, however, and although there would be many retail temptations it would be another lesson. It's absolutely possible to enjoy a city without crashing the cards. There was one area that hadn't made the cut for the press trip itinerary – St Pauli. Not only did it have the recommendation of people who had lived in the city, there were four good reasons I wanted to explore the area: John, Paul, George, and Ringo. In fact five and we need to change that to John, Paul, George, Pete, and Stuart.

The Beatles were just one of many young bands from the UK who had been sent to Hamburg at the birth of the 1960s to play in nightclubs, but they were the only one anyone really cares about now. Knowing that the clubs were close to Reeperbahn, I took off on the pilgrimage. Reeperbahn is long, extremely long in fact, and at points not a place that anyone without a fistful of notes and a slightly soiled raincoat wants to be. The men loitering outside the sex shows and touting for custom ignored me as there was no money to be made, but it was still uncomfortable.

From one doorway spilled eight guys, decked out in fancy dress of lederhosen and Tyrolean hats, each one with his zip down – it was obvious that what they were showing one another wasn't uncooked bratwurst. Clearly inebriated to the point of stupor, they were making loud and disgusting aspersions about the cleanliness of girls who had just been, well performing. It was 11am. While hoping that the girls in question had emptied the men's manky pockets of as many Euros as possible, it was still a sickening site, all the more so when hearing their accents and realising we hailed from the same small island. From that point I wanted to get off this street as quickly as possible so headed off the Reeperbahn and abandoned that day's Beatles' expedition.

The road took me down to the waterfront – a place that in any destination never fails to make me happy. Hamburg made me happy. It's a city with genuine character and would need at least six months to get under its skin. If money hadn't been an issue I would have been happy to visit a bar, order a proper beer, and practise my German.

The next day started extremely early with a quick sidestep to visit the handsome city of Lübeck just to the north, but later in the afternoon I was more prepared for the sights that Reeperbahn might throw up. Instead of wandering blindly, I now knew the addresses of the sites associated with The Beatles. If there were any fears that these would be somehow gentrified, with swarms of tourists, then these were dashed even at Beatles Platz, a square at the top of Große Freiheit, where the clubs they played at are located. It's a bleak expanse for such a celebration, with metal cut-out sculptures of the five. There's also a sign in a pretty grubby window to commemorate the band recording with Bert Kaempfert.

At Große Freiheit 39 the Star Club once stood, but now a plaque hidden up an alleyway pays tribute to many of the bands that played there. Across at number 36 is where the Kaiserkeller stood and further along at no 64 is the Indra, the first place they played.

At the Indra it's particularly easy to imagine them, clad in black leather, taking gear from a van through the narrow doorway for another night of pumping out their versions of the current rock'n'roll favourites.

Around the corner, in a building that is almost consumed by ivy, is the former Bambi cinema where they lived. A small faded sign can be found by scrabbling through the heavy growth – it's a simple black and white framed picture which says *Hier Wohnten Die Beatles 1960*. If this area has been at all cleaned up since they were here as fresh-faced lads, then no wonder Lennon felt this was where he became a man. Having known musicians from Dundee who came over here as young rockers in the early 60s, thinking of them roaming these back streets made me smile.

The Beatles pilgrimage had been successful in The End – fans will get that. There was no other reason to linger in this area, so it was straight into the U Bahn and a few hours of wandering the Colonnaden and soaking in that laidback ambience that German cities somehow manage to maintain, despite their size.

From Hamburg, the plan was to sail from Lübeck to Helsinki then work my way back west through Scandinavia, but the sailing was full for the next few days so that idea was abandoned. Plan B involved the most travelling of any day so far, boarding an early train at Hamburg and travelling through Denmark then Sweden and arriving in Oslo around 10pm. It made sense, believe me.

Better to ask twice
than to lose your way once.

Danish proverb

OCCASIONALLY THE INTERRAIL phone app made planning journeys too easy. Friends who had travelled at the age when most people take off on these adventures had used a large, heavy, bulky European timetable to find out routes and times. Of course, that didn't need to be electronically charged. Consulting the app, the good news was that no additional reservations were required for this full day travelling from Hamburg to Oslo. On the first leg to Copenhagen, it was a short step from feeling stupidly excited about the prospect of travelling through Scandinavia for the first time, to feeling stupid. A kindly and bewhiskered ticket inspector checked the Interrail pass and then asked for my reservation. You know that feeling. The cold, slightly clammy one that descends when it's obvious this isn't going to go well. It seemed the rules had changed recently and a reservation on this leg was required but that was OK, I could pay the 10 Euros or the equivalent in Danish Krone.

Except I couldn't. As the next three countries I was due to visit didn't use the Euro, I didn't replenish the stocks. I was only passing through Denmark so I didn't have Krone. I would withdraw Norwegian currency when I arrived.

I had seven Euros and 60 cents and no Danish currency so offered my card in the futile hope that he would whisk a machine from his back pocket. He shook his head but disappeared for a while, perhaps to give me some time to fumble down the back of seats to raise the required two Euros 40. He knew I wasn't a full-on fare dodger, just a bit daft, and with some wizardry he managed to concoct some form of ticket that would equate to my remaining Euros, satisfy him, and any further inspections on the journey. His responsibilities were over at Puttgarten, however, where the train boarded the ferry that would take us to Denmark. That's right. The train boarded the ferry. This is not geekery, but this was seriously cool and a part of this journey that I hadn't considered. Of course I knew there were stretches of water, but presumed there would be a bridge or a tunnel.

On board the ferry we left the train at a teeny tiny platform and headed up for the 45-minute crossing, enough time to break out the picnic purchased in Hamburg. The loaf that had looked brioche-like on the shelf was actually a light golden exterior masking a black heart of pure dark rye. No plastic camping knife would breach this crust, but at least with this hunk of baked goods, I did have a deadly weapon. With two trains remaining until Oslo, a limited budget and an early no-breakfast start, I delved, spoon first, into a small pot of soft cheese.

Reboarding the train on the ferry was thrilling, but became confusing when someone was in my seat and the backpack disappeared. This time, it wasn't my skewed sense of direction. The guy was slumped in the seat; a menacing school bully at the back of the class. The glare said *I dare you. Ask me to move.* I didn't. Locating the backpack at the end of the carriage, I zipped it open and had a quick look to see that nothing had gone (or been added). From my new seat, I could see him. All he needed was a quiff and a flick knife.

The Danish inspector, a Santa-type figure was given the same treatment when he asked for his ticket. Without looking up, he muttered that it was on his phone. His phone, he slurred, was over there, pointing into the middle distance. Santa was becoming a little agitated and demanded the ticket or money. When those requests were ignored, he stepped up the demand to a passport or papers. With no response to this he told the school bully that he had to get off at the next station. Why was *I* terrified? The guy had slumped further into the seat and smirked.

The spectacle brought the other passengers together, exchanging glances and wondering how this would play out. What followed was a farcical chase through the carriages by two train guards until he was bundled off at a rural station, where he promptly crossed the platform and boarded a waiting train travelling in the opposite direction.

When the trains are clean, comfortable, and on time, only fellow passengers can provide any diversion. Reading requires concentration, music was too much of a distraction, and I needed to buy more notebooks in Copenhagen.

This second leg of the journey, to Gothenburg, would cross the Ørseund Bridge to Malmö, and head north. Opposite was a young woman, about 19 or 20, who through most of the journey concentrated on taking not-so-subtle self-portraits. It seemed there is another universal language – the pout with simultaneous cheek suck. Alongside me was a giant Goth Squirrel, dressed from head to toe in black including fingernails and lips. She would take a tiny amount of nuts and raisins from a plastic container and nibble from her forefingers, quietly and diligently.

Sometimes countryside is dull. Stations are welcome breaks from the never-ending greenness, providing colour and character, so half an hour in Gothenburg was a welcome relief. Not long enough to get out of the station and have even a brief peek, but enough to stretch out and be grateful that this was the final leg to Oslo.

Approaching the platform was a shiny black train. Of course it wasn't mine, it was the glamorous night train to Stockholm, but this admiration for a train was a slight worry, particularly following the swoon over the train-ferry miracle. Waiting to board the less pretty, but still welcome Oslo train, there was a solo female with a massive backpack. She had things dangling from it – the kind of accoutrements that told her back story of serious camping and hostelling. Was I being too careful? I was sticking to a small budget but should I try to hostel again? She looked interesting, though, and had clearly thought a jangle of bangles was essential packing. She looked in my direction but didn't notice I was there. When I caught my reflection I understood. I looked like a giant potato – beige and shapeless with the black backpack providing the potato with an oversized eye. Why would anyone think I had anything interesting to say if I couldn't even choose a colour?

On board, the area around the seat needed a bit of exploration. Do Norwegian trains have phone chargers like their Danish neighbours? What's that in the seat pocket in front? Oh, it's a sick bag. When the train started to rise and fall like a gentle fairground ride, it was understandable. The fact that not much more than half a pot of soft cheese had passed my lips that day was a blessing. The brick of bread had been discarded at Gothenburg station – with a massive clang.

The train tilted and weaved through the countryside, one moment in the middle of the countryside then next to a busy road. The bag didn't come into play, but there were a few empty wrappers from the heave-relieving ginger chews by the end of the line.

One young Finn was intent on finding the title of a song and lurched through carriages, still carrying his lager and giving passengers a full face of its fumes as he sang a few lines. Another guard was given a workout, chasing him up and down the train and insisting he sit down. He forgot the shut up bit unfortunately.

With a slight delay at the border, it was 10.30pm before the train reached Oslo.

The strongest man in the world
is he who stands most alone.

Henrik Ibsen

A WET AND WINDY night, the city's rain-soaked pavements were illuminated by the multi-coloured neon advertising signs signs crowning the buildings.

If anything, the modern budget hotel allows solo travellers to be more detached than ever. An e-mail was sent automatically after booking. It contained a code to print out a key card on arrival. No human interaction required. Staff were on site to deal with any problems and could be reached by using an intercom in the lobby, but this was a ghost hotel with vending machines providing the only bit of warmth. It did, however, have a marvellous heated floor in the bathroom.

Following the close call on the train to Copenhagen, every reservation was double checked. The next train would take the scenic route from Oslo to Bergen, so the first stop in the morning had to be the train station to make sure I had a seat. Scenic should have said it all. Even with three trains a day, the options were limited. Either I would be leaving tomorrow at 3.25pm, or not for another four days.

It was 9am so there was just north of a day and a half to explore, but the fact that I had to leave the next day meant that the money already paid to the hotel for the following night was lost. But I DID have to leave the next day. There wasn't the time or cash to add another two nights in Scandinavia.

Looking ahead to the step after Bergen, which would be a ferry to the northern tip of Denmark, the 1.30pm departure would mean two booking nights in Bergen if I wanted to see anything at all. Once I had booked the cheapest accommodation I could find and a deck ticket on the ferry, I had £40 until the house money dropped.

It was due to come through in four days. I had a debit but no credit card – a result of the past few years' financial problems. It could be done. I

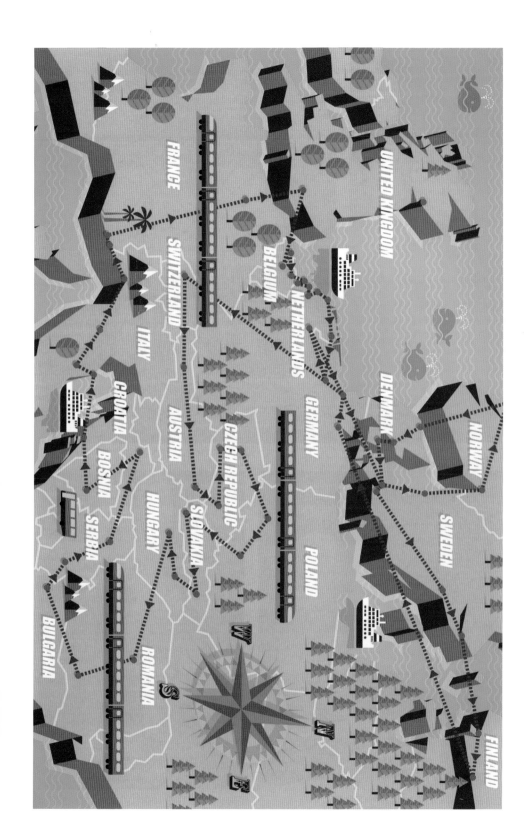

Potato love in Bruges   Quite an arrival at Antwerp Station

Last dance in Rotterdam   Ninja Nintje (Miffy) in Utrecht

Quiet life on the
canal in Haarlem

Preparing to encounter
the non-dangerous
sheep of Texel

More bicycle
nightmares at the
university building
in Groningen

In Celle with cousin
Sonja and Mekki

Shadows of The Beatles
in Hamburg

The Pillow Man
welcomes
solo travellers
in Oslo

Snowing in June on the journey from Oslo to Bergen

Early morning arrival at Hirthsals

Cool commune living in Aarhus

Tivoli lights the darkness in Copenhagen

In the footsteps of Hans Christian Andersen in Odense

The hunt for the Øresund Bridge at Malmö - it's there, honestly...

Looking to
the future in
Norrköping

Preparing to
be Agnetha in
Stockholm

Daisy sculpture
in Turku

Helsinki Station (below) and living it up on the Baltic Sea ferry

Freddie Mercury lives large on the shores of Lake Montreux

The arcades of Bern

Feeling 13 years old again in Interlaken

hadn't made a habit of fine dining so could eat from supermarkets. Glad that I hadn't beaten myself up, not too badly anyway, I was heartened that for once I could stop, think, and see the big picture. The only thing to do today was look at the map, make a plan, get lost, find out where I was, and delve into the city, horizontal rain or not.

However, Thor smiled on me, the clouds parted, and the skies turned bright blue. Wandering through Grünnerløkka, the bohemian area of the city, a sense of euphoria gave me the massive hug that only wonderful experiences can. From the hair shirt of the hotel room to the joy of clambering across the roof of the Oslo Opera House (it's OK – it's designed for that) blinded by the snow-white architecture against the bright sun, it's amazing how life can change when we can give ourselves a shake.

Even a fortress was exciting that day. Never normally someone who would cross the road to look at a cannon, the Akershus Castle and Fortress proved to be the perfect place for a wander and some preconception busting. Perched high above the harbour it is still used for high-profile events, with a permanent concert stage within its walls.

In the Norwegian Resistance Museum, also in the grounds, there is a stirring image of the Norwegian Resistance Movement striding up the cobbles to retake the fortress from the country's Nazi occupiers. Traitors including Vidkun Quisling, head of the Norwegian Nazis, were executed here a few months after the end of the Second World War.

Apart from the history, I was unusually fascinated by the modern sculpture trail with every piece designed by schoolchildren. On a bench was The Pillow Man, a seated figure in stainless steel. The sign alongside said that anyone sitting on the bench could never be alone. The Pillow Man would be a friend. I had to reach under my glasses – must have been something in my eye.

Wandering the streets of Oslo it seemed that other visitors didn't realise that I was one of them – and had no sense of direction. Blonde hair, fair skin, and light blue eyes might have pointed to me as a local but I had to say, *sorry, I don't live here,* so often that it struck me – apart from a few months, this was the first time since the age of 22 that I had no home of my own.

Now someone else was in the shower that I had chosen. They were walking over the patio that had been laid by my friend Rod the previous year, during the last weeks of Kali's life. They were hot and perfect for a tiny sun worshipper like her.

There was no sadness about never going back there, but I tried to retain the good memories. Still, I was conscious that my life had changed beyond recognition – my next home would be a rented flat, somewhere high above Abu Dhabi.

The offer of a job had come at the right time. After five years when money was the biggest worry, this could be a couple of years when money was the least of my worries. Being careful, I could be back on a firm financial footing relatively quickly.

Wandering through residential areas, the buildings painted in subtle colours with beautiful wrought-iron balconies and each with a unique doorway, became the next dream home. This was happening too often but when rootless, life can be projected anywhere with nothing from home intruding – no sofas, beds, curtains, or cutlery. I had none of those. I knew where my stuff was, but that was someone else's home and that's liberating and terrifying in equal measure.

Looking back on myself as a teenager, the traditional path of job, marriage, kids didn't really cross my mind. Thank goodness. I would have been sorely disappointed if that had been the ambition. Work had always been fine, the marriage was a disaster, and the girl plumbing had just never worked. If my 18-year-old self looked ahead at her life to see this, what would she think? Loser? Stupid? Oddball? None of it mattered really. The cards were dealt up to this point, I just had to play the hand I was given. At the moment it was solitaire.

But I was in awesome Oslo. The evening was bright and sunny again, with the Aker Brygge area lined with packed bars and restaurants. The budget wouldn't allow a quick glass of white down here, but it didn't matter. Walking down as far as the Astrup Fearnley Museum of Modern Art, a public swimming area served these cleanly designed apartments that were a world away from traditional Grünnerløkka, but still as much of a dream home.

The next morning came with a realisation that, apart from a takeaway sandwich, I had spent close to zero Euros the day before so I had some wiggle room to invest in a little culture. Even the walk to the National Gallery gave my heart cause to soar a little. Feeling buoyed I brandished a student card for the reduced entrance fee, even though I was on a break from the course – desperate times and all that. At least it wasn't an outright fib – I could have claimed to be studying art and been given completely free entry.

Like most foreign visitors, the main reason to visit was to see The Scream by Edvard Munch. Unlike most, I didn't make a beeline for the gallery in which it hung and didn't curse the fact that no photographs were allowed. Perhaps it's one of those images that is so parodied that the original has lost its power, but it was completely underwhelming in the canvas, as it were.

Maybe it's an art thing. My attempts at committing visual ideas to paper are generally met with approval – if raucous laughter is approval.

There was time for one more treat before the Bergen train. Somewhere I felt on safer ground. At the Henrik Ibsen Museum, his apartment is open for guided tours – they used to be self-guided until visitors started making off with souvenirs. The group was made up of a Scot, an American, a Slovenian, and two Uruguayans – quite a reach for any playwright. The apartment was fairly modest and tasteful. The museum has everything from his coat, top hat and cane to theatre memorabilia and his small travelling bag. He was publicity shy, but would stroll down to the Grand Café every morning. His celebrity led to some of the first paparazzi shots, with photographers finding ways to disguise camera equipment under overcoats.

Even though my time in Oslo had been put to good use, I had a deep sadness leaving the city, contenting myself with the prospect of Bergen, a place that trusted sources had said outshone the capital. The platform was packed, but on boarding I feared the seat I had been assigned was back to travel. If it was anything like as stomach-churning as the journey to Oslo even the ginger chews might not prevent the chunder bag being used – this could be more than seven hours of mountainous terrain.

Seats couldn't be booked facing forwards. Generally because they don't know which direction the carriages will arrive from. With a lurch the train moved but it reversed, which meaning I was facing forwards. And relax.

Heading out of Oslo the suburbs appeared to stretch forever, but were still fascinating. Not to the young French couple snogging in the seats in front, sharing my window and my window blind. She decided to pull the blind halfway down to add some mood to their smooches, not ideal for a scenic train. As soon as they unlocked lips long enough for a toilet visit, I snapped the blind back up, all the while looking at her beau, challenging him to stop me. He didn't. My seat partner slept most of the way, which made me think he was local. Who would book this famous scenic journey then use it to get some shut-eye?

As we climbed into the mountains the landscape opened up and a late heavy snowfall lay deep and crisp and dazzlingly white. The landscape was made all the more sensational by the azure skies against the virgin snow, with nothing more than mountain huts painted in traditional dark red, and shiny snowmobiles. At Myrdal station, there was a mass exodus as people joined the line to Flam, where they would travel out to the fjords.

If you look out to the right, you will have some wonderful views, but very quick. Do not look away.

My seat partner had woken up and as I looked round at him he warned me to keep my eyes on the view – it was just a glimpse. This was a taster of what the passengers to Flam would be taking in soon. He was right, each view lasted a few seconds but they were enough to make me wish I had joined that train to Flam.

He was a Bergen native who had been visiting family in Oslo. Hoping for an insider's guide I asked for tips, but they turned out to be what I would find highlighted on the tourist map anyway. Even though it was after 10pm when we arrived, it was still light. The hostel was only 10 minutes' walk away and the street was located with remarkable ease. Chuffed. Not for long though. The photograph on the booking site seemed to match a completely different building. Looking around for someone to ask, the only people on the street were two burly security guys on the door of a lively, and by lively I mean slightly scary, bar. They pointed upstairs, which I didn't really understand, but it seemed that the hostel was located above this delightful hostelry and, as it was after normal reception hours, check-in was at the bar.

For a week night in Bergen the bikers were out in force and a 40-something woman in a fleece and backpack cut something of a strange figure among the black furniture, black floors, and black lips and fingernails. It had a whiff of Rocky Horror to it. At any moment Frank n Furter would come out from behind the bar and show me to the room. Riff Raff was collecting glasses.

The barmaid had paperwork to complete but the decibels meant that no further discussion was happening. When I had booked, a finger slip meant the two nights had been booked separately. I couldn't check at that point whether I could stay in the same room for both nights but there was laundry to do and I didn't fancy moving damp smalls from room to room.

Four flights later the room was, well it was there. The corridor had that olde worlde asylum charm. The room was a riot of brown and everything had a slight layer of stickiness, bringing barefoot bravery to an end. The communal kitchen seemed relatively clean until I opened the fridge with the intention of storing food. It came back to the room, along with the stench of whatever had been left in the fridge for, well, forever it seemed. I went to bed and dreamed of characterless and clean rooms, reminding myself that this place was cheap, well it wasn't cheap but it was cheap for Bergen.

Before heading out the next morning the room situation needed to be sorted. Reception opened at 10am so I headed down to the lobby. The desk was still shuttered and a Japanese family were also waiting, not patiently, checking the time every couple of minutes and shouting at one another.

With check-out at 11 I had to wait, but at 10.30 a young woman, lost in music it seemed, sauntered past and sat behind the shutters for a couple of minutes before the family rattled her cage. She took out one earphone and looked up without moving her head, unperturbed by their rage. The shutters were raised and she dealt with everything within five minutes before reconnecting with her tunes. I could stay in my caramel-coloured and textured abode.

With my finely tuned sense of direction it was wise to seek out the ferry port for the next day, even though it only 15 minutes' walk away on an allegedly straightforward route. Knowing that I wouldn't be running towards the boat as it disappeared towards the horizon allowed me to enjoy the day ahead. It was a strange morning, with grey skies dampening my mood and nothing in Bergen pushing the button that lifted me into enthusiasm, never mind euphoria. Maybe it was the crowds, with the tour group ducklings jostling anyone who crossed their path. Even the beauty of the fifteenth-century Brygge area was slightly underwhelming, the proliferation of souvenir emporiums made Bergen feel like Blackpool reimagined in Farrow & Ball paint colours.

The Brygge is a UNESCO Heritage Site but looks so perfect that it's almost theme-parkish. Beyond the multi-coloured facades the narrow back courts were more interesting however, housing artists and craftspeople doing brisk trade.

Away from the Brygge, the narrow busy streets meant tourists shared limited pavement space, bringing us close enough to eavesdrop, and for me a chance to embrace the fact that I was alone and could make my own decisions. Two women, either partners or friends, were showing all the signs of being together for too long. The discussion concerned which side of the street they should walk on. A discussion that became slightly heated, then frosty, then heated, then resigned. They stayed on the same side, but I was tempted to suggest they take a side each, giving them something to discuss at dinner later – if they ever managed to choose a venue.

Even though cash was limited, there was no way I could take food back to the hostel. Finding somewhere cheap would be difficult here, but I was encouraged by a message that the house money should land in my account the following day. A sparsely filled roll and a bottle of lingonberry juice were the healthy choice but also took pounds off my purse. I managed to stretch it through a heavy rain shower and spent the rest of the day in the grounds of the Bergenhus Fortress with its pretty courtyards, then strolling the streets on the opposite side of the harbour. I warmed to the place as the day progressed but it didn't capture my heart as Oslo had.

The next day, before checking in for the late afternoon ferry, I decided to go a little off-piste and found a Bergen that still didn't knock Oslo off its pedestal but made me understand why friends had recommended it so highly. Roaming up and down the streets of the hilly residential area close to the port was not only superb exercise, particularly with a backpack, but allowed a little more dream home fantasising. It also encouraged me to revisit the more touristy areas, which I seemed to look upon more kindly.

The money still hadn't dropped so there was still a slight churn in my stomach. Once I boarded the ferry there would be no internet connection unless I paid for it – but I couldn't afford to do that. The crossing was overnight but the difference between a cabin and what they described as an airline seat was enough that budget trumped comfort. Walking on board after a slick check-in, there was an army of us foot passengers. I knew the first stop had to be the luggage lockers to make sure the backpack could be stowed for the journey. This left me with the waist pack, which could stretch to also accommodate a kindle, iPod, and rudimentary toiletries.

For an hour at least, passengers shuffled aimlessly through the upper decks. These contained the entertainment – cafés, bars, video games, and gambling. The second priority was to check the menus and how much a coffee would cost me. Not knowing if the money had dropped, the small amount I had left needed to be kept for emergencies. There was still a chance that once I hit the port at Hirtshals there would be a wait until the account was healthier if I wanted to see Denmark, which I did. Badly. The Interrail pass only had a few days remaining, so the alternative would be to travel straight to Copenhagen, where I could wait it out and buy my next pass whenever the bank account allowed.

Again, I was remarkably sanguine. There was a situation to deal with and I'd deal with it. I wouldn't starve overnight. I had music, I had books to read, there were charging points, and in the morning I'd be in Denmark for the first time. There was still amusement to be had by wandering the decks and poking my head into every bar, hoping that something would grab my attention. The entertainment on offer was not altogether unfamiliar.

Family holidays as a child were always to Blackpool and the Pontin's holiday camp on the outskirts of the town. These were built and run to map out every hour of the day. Being the youngest by almost 11 years, by the time I was old enough to realise we were on holiday my siblings were too old to join us. As a child, there was always something to do, I was never lonely. For my mum and dad, both hard workers, they could arrive and choose whatever suited them from the programme, knowing that I was occupied and safe within the confines of the camp. Looking back it was camp in more ways than one, but as a 10-year-old it was more about talent shows and trampolines. There was no need to escape, everything I needed was there.

There was no escaping here either, but now I was a caged animal who didn't fit with the more mature clientele in the showbar listening to the afternoon singalong and the bingo (although, being in Danish, it was pretty entertaining from the next room), or the glossy smiles of the evening cabaret.

It was ideal dead time to catch up on notes and check when I should send postcards to those who who had pre-ordered the book by funding its first run. Depending on how much they've had to drink, people who spot someone writing in a notebook will either maintain their curiosity at a distance or the interest will start small and escalate. It starts with a smile and then a mime of writing in a notebook and a laugh. It's best to try to avoid eye contact, but still they lurch towards you, thinking that they're doing you a favour. I mean, no woman could possibly want to sit anywhere alone. The attention of a man – any man – must be preferable to that. Then, when they are told that you're happy sitting alone, they are perfectly within their rights to say that a fat woman in glasses should be grateful of any attention she gets. That was pleasant.

The expensive cabin was looking pretty good now, particularly when checking where my airline seat was situated. The passenger in the next seat had already gone to sleep and discarded his boots and socks on my seat. It was going to be a long night.

I knew I could catch up on sleep on the train. If the money had dropped Aarhus was the next destination. If not, well, I'd deal with that.

Later in the evening, with the man in the next airline seat now partially clothed, snoring and drooling, I wasn't going to attempt to squeeze past and clear my chair of his belongings. Staying up all night to write was the only option, fuelled by several cups of strong vending machine coffee. The casualties of the evening's drinking were roaming the decks like cheery zombies, so once again I became a hooch hound magnet. This time it was incomprehensible gobbledygook – a combination of gobbledygook and probably Norwegian or Danish. It was hard to tell. It didn't last. The grog guzzler roared at the air and collapsed, snoring within seconds and making wailing noises in his sleep. Another strange character with Captain Jack Sparrow hair and make-up, but topped off by a tall hat, did circuits of the deck.

I wasn't alone. A couple of night owls were also in the bar and when the reanimated zombie launched himself at them, overturning their table, they called security. When they arrived he had slumped into an even deeper sleep. Security left, content that he wouldn't cause further trouble.

Still Jack Sparrow circled…

When the sun rose I wrapped up as well as my meagre wardrobe allowed and watched the northern tip of Denmark approach. I welcomed the new day. There was just the small matter of what would happen now.

It was 8am at Hirtshals and we disembarked to nothing. The port was just that. No facilities, never mind an ATM. So on this sunny Friday morning I trudged out of the port and towards civilisation. Where were the foot soldiers who had boarded alongside me? It seemed that everyone apart from me and one other man were being ticked off on a clipboard as they boarded coaches.

The train leaving Lillehende station here was on a private line not covered by Interrail. I had enough to get on the train, but I had to know now whether there were further funds. There was no 4G to access mobile data, so there was no option but to walk through these sleepy residential streets and reach the town centre. My hand shook as the PIN number gave up its four beeps. A combination of fatigue and fear. Of course the money was there, the book would be ending now without it, but the sense of relief was thrilling. An emotion that I hadn't experienced before and would rather not again.

With Danish Krone in my wallet, I made my way back to Lillehende and hoped a private train would at least have Wi-Fi so I could make a hotel booking in Aarhus. On the walk I encountered two familiar figures – the wailing carouser and the top-hatted pirate. Together. They approached me, oblivious to having seen me before, and asked if I knew if any bars were open.

They tried English first, which was handy. Neither had any recollection of what had happened during the night. Rather than being embarrassed, they exchanged a hearty high five, with the wailer saying, *Thank goodness it was a Danish boat. I would never have got away with that shit if the boat was Norwegian.* He had also lost his locker key and had to pay 2000 NOK, around £150, to get his luggage back, which appeared to consist of a plastic bag and a sweatshirt.

To travel is to live.

Hans Christian Andersen

IT WAS ONLY 20 minutes from Lillehende to Hjørring and the onward connection to Aarhus. Time passed quickly as I stood in a line of passengers, equally bewildered by the onboard ticket machine. It was only from Hjørring that I could relax, still basking in that warm, soapy, fragrant bath of relief now that I had the cash to carry on.

This also meant some planning was required. Although the capital was a must in Denmark, there were a couple of places en route to Copenhagen that stood out – Aarhus in particular. Being from Dundee, I had been so used to hearing people say they hadn't been to the city or had driven through it that exploring locations outside of the big hitters in Europe was important to me.

The station itself is beautifully understated, but it was disappointing to find the walk to my chosen hotel was via a concrete shopping street, more attractive than some I had encountered but still dotted with rails of cheap clothing. At least they provided some colour. Passing over a couple of bridges, the side streets and smaller squares were visible and raised my expectations.

The accommodation was another budget box, but at least there was a human being to speak with at check-in. A basic and clean room with a shower was all that was required, but finding a private room in a hostel was becoming more difficult as time went on. Perhaps a 12-person dormitory with shared facilities wouldn't have been an issue if I had experienced it at 18.

I had travelled at that age – and travelled alone. A few months after starting my first job at the magazine publisher DC Thomson, I planned a week in London. Booked into a B&B in King's Cross, my friend Kerin joined me on the overnight coach from Dundee. She was enduring a round trip of 1000 miles for a single day at the Horse of the Year Show. At least I was planning a week of cultural goodness.

It was my first time away alone and I was naïve to the point of having no idea why characters hanging around King's Cross were sizing up every lone youngster around the station. The B&B itself was what I regarded at that time as basic; what I recognise now as downright sleazy.

In days when money was more plentiful, but more often on press trips, there had been experiences at the other end of the spectrum, with suites at The Savoy in London, rooms with private terraces on the most beautiful Australian beaches, extravagant rooms at the Waldorf in New York, Nile cruises, twinkly ski lodges in Whistler, and many others. It's not a boast, in fact I look back now and think that some of the trips were pretty vulgar. What it shows is that luxury is far from crucial to the overall experience. Unless the plan is to spend most of the stay in the room, then all that's needed is a comfortable bed, a decent shower, and a good location. Naïve I might have been, but that week in London when I was 19 is one of the best trips I have ever taken. It's all about the new.

It was Friday afternoon and Aarhus had the familiar buzz of anticipation that any city has for the weekend. Tomorrow would be the real expedition; today was a wander, soaking up that buzz. There might have been a beer and an open sandwich involved, but the growing affection for Aarhus meant that a bit of research was carried out that night. I didn't want to miss anything that I would regret later.

Beyond the retail purgatory, Aarhus appeared to be a city reinventing itself through the arts and education and it was the completely fresh experience I was looking for.

On Saturday morning, the breakfast was a five-star buffet for such basic accommodation. The breakfast room was at the top of the hotel and already busy. While there wasn't a piano player who stopped when I walked in, there was still some perplexed looks. Women on their own who aren't in business suits are still seen as unusual. Women who appear to be quite comfortable on their own are seen as even stranger creatures. I was comfortable and took full advantage of the breakfast. I even had thirds.

Heading back along one of those promising streets leading from the main shopping drag, which I now knew was Strøget, the hunt was on for a building that on its own would have made the whole stay worthwhile. Aarhus Town Hall.

Architecture eh? For so long, people who can successfully translate what they have in their head to paper – drawing I think it's called – had made me feel that because my attempts to do that had resulted in something comical it meant that I wasn't creative and didn't have the right to comment on anything visual.

Rubbish of course. The reaction to anything visual doesn't need to come from a position of competence. Since seeing an exhibition featuring Danish designer Arne Jacobsen's work 10 years before, anything I've seen that he designed has made me happy. I don't know why – I don't want to know why. Everything from cutlery to chairs to buildings – it's gorgeous.

And in Aarhus was a building that he designed. When it was built in 1947 it created a bit of a stooshie (Scottish word for uproar, but nothing beats stooshie) due to its modernism. Again, it made me happy, from a distance and even more so up close.

Knowing that Jacobsen's work usually extended to the interiors, I was desperate to see inside. The foyer was simple, elegant, and the only thing I would see. The security guard made it quite clear that the foyer was the end of my pilgrimage.

There was another reason. A wedding party had just arrived. Small and informal, but it was clear that this was their big day. The last thing they needed was a gawking tourist in the background of the pictures. Following the inspection of the foyer, which more than lived up to expectations, I walked around the building to look at it from every possible angle. It made me happy.

By this stage I was straddling the line between tourist and hobo chic. Without any attempt, I had been losing weight. Food had been less of a priority and walking had been the best way to see every location. Due to the lack of cash up to that point, I hadn't bought a smaller size of trousers. The current pair were increasingly clown-like and either needed a belt or to be left in Aarhus. They were left in a textile recycling bin.

Aside from Arne's town hall, there was pretty unanimous opinion at the hotel reception desk that Den Gamle By – the old town – had to be visited. This wasn't an old town as we know it. It certainly wasn't a network of well-preserved old streets and traditional shops. Well it was. In a way. Den Gamle By is an open-air museum that was founded before some of the exhibits. It was founded in 1909 to preserve Danish building from the 18th and 19th centuries that would have otherwise disappeared under the developer's bulldozer. The buildings were brought here and reassembled in a village setting.

It has continued to develop and now the journey starts in the 18th century, moves through the 19th and into the last century, with recreations of the 1920s and an ever-expanding and groovy recreation of 1970s Denmark. The streets are lined with shops, bars, pubs, and even a jazz club. There are cars from the time and the exact re-creation of an apartment building from

1974 Aarhus, featuring stories of the original occupants – everyone from an elderly single woman to a hippy commune; even a gynaecologist's office. This is history that everyone can relate to (and those who can't can point and laugh) with exhibitions of vintage clothing and the incredible Aarhus Rocks!, a celebration of Denmark's centre of rock and pop, with everything from teenagers' bedrooms to recording studios. If there was an eighth heaven, I was there.

There was one more stop before Copenhagen.

Odense, the main city on the island of Funen, was less than two hours away. It has a huge selling point – maybe not huge, but extremely tall. Everywhere, even on the paving stones, there is a reminder that this was the city that gave us Hans Christian Andersen. That was a good enough reason for any writer to stop off.

The hotel was next to the station and part of the same chain used in Aarhus, so there were no surprises, apart from the separate slip of paper I was handed at reception after being given the once over. This informed me that any vomit found in the room would incur a cleaning cost of 500 Danish Krone. I like my continental lager, but what had they heard?

The sun had come out again and there were certainly more young people than I expected sitting on the street, all drinking beer with backpacks at their feet – did HC Andersen have something of a hardcore following?

From the room window I could see a poster that covered the entire side of a building, and showing the Tinderbox Festival was in town, or just outside of town. The hotel was obviously hosting festival-goers who were being poured off the buses from the site full of the sponsor's brew. More important though, they looked at me and decided that I could be one of those drunken nuisances who would come back wrecked. I still had it. I could still be there in the depths of the mosh pit 'rocking out' to… who was headlining anyway? Robbie Williams.

The rest of the bill, with bands like The Cardigans, was enough to consider trying for a ticket but the Sunday had SOLD OUT written through the date. Maybe it was just as well. A few Danish brews, no sense of direction, and the bus would be off without me.

There was no easy way to get lost in Hans Christian's Odense. Just follow his large bronze footprints to the sights associated with his life here, including the museum built on the site of his childhood home. In parts it was as magical as some of his creations, but it was the story of the man and his own travels that was captivating. They have his personal library and part of the cottage where he lived as a child is accessed through the museum. There are also extravagant art exhibits re-creating stories like The Princess and the Pea and The Emperor's New Clothes. Just fantastical. And they have his false teeth. Less so, but still a great part of the story.

Of course there is more to Odense, but in reality there doesn't need to be. This was a Sunday, a day when families were walking prams, toddlers, and the inevitable small dog along the river. It was properly lazy, properly relaxing, and how anyone hooked on Danish TV series such as *Borgen* imagines the super-cool Danes spending a Sunday. Even though I wasn't part of any groups, I could integrate myself into this scene. Alone but not lonely – ideal.

In a quiet square away from the river, a corner restaurant called Grønttorvet was serving a traditional Danish buffet lunch. It wasn't cheap and there were only a couple of things that looked delicious enough to invest, so I decided that after such a decent breakfast, a beer wasn't going to do too much damage. As long as it was local it was research, so a glass of Odense it was.

The bars in the strangely named Latin Quarter began to fill up with Tinderbox punters who hadn't hung around for Robbie, but it was time to head back and prepare for a couple of days in *Wonderful Wonderful Copenhagen*. After Aarhus and Odense, it had a lot to live up to.

Remember we're all
in this alone.

Lily Tomlin

ARRIVING AT COPENHAGEN station once again, I could leave the building this time. The benefit of quieter destinations was apparent immediately. From sleepy Odense it was just 90 minutes before my backpack was one among hundreds, along with small suitcases, large suitcases, and bustling crowds heading into a busy Monday afternoon. It was so busy that it was difficult to see any of the city's famous charm. The backpack was heavy with purchases and postcards to post, so the hostel was a priority.

It was part of a chain that is raising the game of hostelling in major European cities. Large, clean, bright and, can I use this word, funky, there appeared to be a mix of single people, couples, groups, and even families. This is the acceptable face of hostelling for many, morphing into budget accommodation but still with ultra-cheap dorms for the hardened hostellers or those with no other choice. The private rooms are basic and plastic, with pod-type bathrooms. No air conditioning, but there are windows, and no TV, but that's a good thing. The Wi-Fi is free and fast and easy. Perfect.

It was 30 minutes' walk from the station and the heat was building. I had definite plans for that evening so decided to pace the day, despite the girlish excitement of being here for the first time. Again, the Odense breakfast had been good and substantial so food wasn't a priority. This eating when hungry was a new thing and I liked it.

Following a *Borgen* pilgrimage to the parliament building of Christiansborg Palace, to see where my favourite TV show of the past 10 years had been filmed, the Danish Architecture Centre was a place to hide from blazing sun – I had forgotten the lucky sunhat and wasn't risking sunstroke.

Denmark was proving to be my ideal destination. The evening was comfortably warm with a sun that wasn't nearly ready to set, but was providing the most calming light.

There was another Arne Jacobsen building to see. It was near the station and close to that evening's main destination, the Tivoli Gardens. I had seen Jacobsen's SAS Radisson Hotel towering over other buildings when I arrived, but I knew that the interior would be even better.

Arriving at the SAS, I stopped outside and caught sight of those who were already drinking in the bar and eating in the restaurant. Then I then saw my own reflection. Who was I kidding? I couldn't rock up to the bar looking like this.

Well I could, but I didn't feel worthy. I was a 13-year-old chubby school-girl again, hiding in the corner of the school disco, wearing clothes that her mum had bought for her and watching friends have their first slow dances. In hindsight it's ridiculous but for that moment I was the Dickensian urchin with her nose pressed up against the sweet shop window.

Snapping back into practical mode, it made sense to drop into the station and buy the next Interrail pass. The queue was lengthy but it provided some time to cheer up before heading into the Tivoli Gardens. Reaching the sales desk after two and a half hours I was more chipper and decided that I would take the plunge and buy the two passes that would take me right through to the beginning of September.

The Tivoli Gardens are next to the station, with high walls giving no real clue as to what lies within, apart from a couple of rides that poke up beyond the height of the walls. The lighting here is famous and the idea was to see the park illuminated after sundown.

Taking my place in the queue behind a young couple, I could hear them discuss every possible permutation of ticket, then tried to tell the man in the booth why it would make more economic sense to charge for every ride separately rather than as an all-in-one ticket, either with or without rides... Then they left.

My ticket was without the rides. Without knowing it, the beautiful people of Copenhagen, drinking and being stylish in the SAS, had knocked my confidence and I couldn't see myself standing in a queue to be strapped in to a thrill ride alone.

The Gardens are an old-style amusement park with pavilions, beautifully designed cafés and restaurants, as well as ponds, pagodas, and some more modern high-speed rides alongside the strutting peacocks and candy floss. I can't remember when I last felt so alone. Amusement parks are not for the solo traveller. This is fun to be shared. However, the 99 Krone had been paid. Trying to jolly the mood, I bought an ice-cream. With my creamy cool friend in hand I sat in one of the deckchairs near the front of the large stage where over the summer major acts would play – but not tonight. I had just missed Snoop Dogg – there are always things to be grateful for.

As far as the eye could see, people were in groups, together. There wasn't another solo reveller in sight. Forgetting about the errant incisor, the first crunch of waffle cone dislodged it, leading to a quick extraction and hiding it in the, by now, usual safe place. The ice-cream had melted, leaving an attractive trail down my front. People were looking, I didn't imagine it. It wasn't pleasant but I held my head high, found the ladies room to clean myself up and replaced the tooth as well as I could.

There was a while to wait until the lights came on, so the best plan was to use the time to take some notes, as cheery as they would be. With no pen, it was time to browse the souvenir shops. The first one was £10 but it did light up in water. The second, a standard ballpoint, was a mere £4, but it did have Københaven written along the side. It was that or a giant souvenir pencil… Writing notes (again, weird lady) would at least keep me occupied for the next 90 minutes until it was due to get dark.

Then I saw her. She was sitting alone, relaxing on a deckchair with not a care in the world. Munching on popcorn, she wasn't looking around, she wasn't uncomfortable, she seemed to be enjoying the stillness – I could learn a lot from her.

Then her male counterpart appeared and she exploded. *Where the hell have you been? How long does it take to go to the toilet? How could you have lost me? I've been right here!* Ah well.

I couldn't relax enough to take many photographs that night. I felt like an oddball being alone here. I wasn't going to compound that by taking pictures with so many children around. But I dug my heels in to see those lights – even decent dusk would do. As soon as it became dark enough for the gardens to twinkle, there was one more circuit of the park to take them all in – and they were exquisite.

Heading back through the city to the hostel was heady at night. It was balmy and busy and, now that the melancholy of the Tivoli had passed, that overwhelming rush of being alone in a new city came back. Maybe there were some places that didn't suit the solo traveller, but so many more did.

By the time morning came I was practically skipping. Maybe the evening hadn't lived up to the afternoon, but learning how to deal with disappointment was worthwhile.

With that behind me, money in my wallet, and no breakfast at the hostel, it was time for a treat. The choice along Nyhavn was endless, but having settled on a corner café bar called Nyhavn 17, I didn't look too closely at the prices and ordered what might be called the works. The waitress was English, studying here for her Masters. An English couple seated behind me were delighted to hear her accent, asking her if she wouldn't just bring them proper tea but also make it for them as she would be the only one who would know how.

It was a languorous, sunny, blissful breakfast watching crowds amble harbourside. Leaving the waitress a generous tip – in many ways I wished I was her age again and had that kind of opportunity – I repositioned the lucky hat to shield my eyes from the already strong sun and headed to the southern part of the city.

Even though Copenhagen is a capital city, most places that a short-break visitor will want to see can be reached on foot, with a little effort perhaps. There are many cyclists of course, but less predatory than in previous destinations.

Heading into the area known as the Freetown of Christiania, it's clear that you're not in Copenhagen any more Toto. It feels like its own city, because it almost is. Since squatters took over demilitarised buildings in the Christianhavn area in 1971 there have been 35 years of protracted discussion about its status. But it's still there and operates under a special law that shifted how it's governed from city to state.

It started with the hippies and developed into a community for people who live what's called an alternative lifestyle by those who don't understand that everyone's life is unique. We all live alternative lifestyles to one another.

There are around 900 people living there, with half of the 760 adults working in Copenhagen and the bulk of the rest operating the shops, cafés, and artists' studios in Christiania itself. The residents pay taxes for the usual services, but all decisions here are by made by consensus.

For many people it's the area where marijuana, while not legal, is tolerated and sold openly. The large signs at the entrances to what is called the Green Light Zone are hand-painted but crystal clear – NO PHOTOS. The main drag is called Pusher Street, where hash and weed are sold with the express understanding from authorities that any other drugs are completely off-limits. How do I know all this? From a tour I overheard. Sitting on a low wall with a falafel, a tour group sat alongside me while their guide, one of the first residents, told the whole story. What should I do? Chip in? Or would that single me out as a breadhead, er, man?

There was never any possibility of buying anything on Pusher Street. I wouldn't know what to do with it. I'm not saying I haven't tried it – but I can't smoke and don't really want to practise enough to become proficient. Those trying to coach me through it have enjoyed a great deal of mirth as their reward. It was enough to have a beer at the open-air bar, watch those around me pass their purchases around, and decline politely when they offered to include me.

From the brightly painted walls and mellow frenzy of Christiania, the stroll back through the city confirmed that the city was my newest passion. If I had walked away from Arne Jacobsen last night, he was bound to be at the Danish Design Museum. In a ridiculously pretty building, the contents were enough to keep me out of the afternoon sun for several hours. And here he was. An extensive selection of his chairs and many other pieces were kept together in the Arne Jacobsen room. Next time, I'd have a cocktail in his bar at the SAS. A late afternoon snack of mushrooms on toast in the museum café was the closest I would get to a mood-altering substance that day.

An evening walk to find one of the city's most famous landmarks took me past a hulking cruise ship. The passengers were back on board for the evening's sailing – a German gentleman (I could hear him shouting) who had maybe been taking advantage of an all-inclusive drinks package stood up on his balcony and exposed himself. Deliberate or not, he found it hysterically funny.

A short stroll further on, The Little Mermaid was a small and underwhelming sight, with the walk to and from the statue more enjoyable than seeing her in situ. Back down for an evening at Nyhavn, I sat with a cold beer at the top end of the harbour and enjoyed a blissful summer evening. I would be back, but I wouldn't be alone.

My path has not been determined.
I shall have more experiences and pass many more milestones.

Agnetha Fältskog

THE SECOND trip across the Øresund Bridge was the one that mattered. The choice of route took me across twice, so the first was something of a recce. This time, I would actually get off at Malmö. The bridge is only open to traffic, with trains running below the road, so it doesn't provide expansive views as it crosses the Øresund Strait between Denmark and Sweden, but it does provide a few glimpses of shots used in the opening credits of *The Bridge*. This marvel of bridge engineering has become better known as the concept behind a Scandinavian police series, albeit a pretty incredible one.

I know someone who lives in Malmö – a good friend of my ex-partner – but I hadn't seen him and his wife for 10 years and feared that dropping a note saying I was in town might be met by tumbleweed. The solitary lifestyle was working out for the majority of the time and, besides, I was on a mission.

Crowdfunding any project includes offering rewards to pledgers. For this book, some generous souls pledged considerably higher amounts than necessary to cover their pre-order of the book. For that, they were offered more than a book and a postcard. They were also sent a souvenir from the location of their choice.

My friend Shenagh, in her usual forthright way, said she didn't care what it was but anything connected to the Øresund Bridge would be great. It appeared that neither the Danes nor Swedes realised the potential they had for tourist tat or even a bit of Scandi Cool collectable here. There were some postcards that looked like stills from a 1970s public information film, which is strange considering the bridge opened in 2000.

Shenagh is an important person in my life. Constantly supportive, but not in an unquestioning way. Wise and funny and caring, if she wanted something connected to the Øresund Bridge, she would damn well have it. Some of the photographs I had been taking weren't half bad, so the idea was to get close to the bridge, take some arty photos and have them framed for her. The next morning would be the Hunt for the Øresund Bridge.

On arrival in Malmö, once the backpack was deposited at the hotel, there was the customary recce, which wasn't spectacular, revealing a city that was pretty but unremarkable. However, it had the most architecturally impressive budget supermarket I had ever seen.

The hotel had the cheeriest receptionist ever and was part of the city's concert hall, its corridors lined with posters. The price was a little higher than I would have liked but this was full-on trouser press land with CNN and tea and coffee-making facilities. Breakfast was included too, with the familiar stares. It wasn't women who were staring, however, it tended to be the male half of couples. When the female turned to see what they were looking at, she was satisfied that he wasn't looking with anything apart from curiosity.

The next morning was baking hot, but I would be walking near the waterfront, dominated by the Turning Torso, a 57-storey building with offices and apartments and a distinctive twisted shell that pierces the blue sky. The route towards the bridge was in the opposite direction, along the Ribersborgsstranden. The beaches have beautifully designed jetties and piers with expanses of grass behind, where families were picnicking after spending time on the sands.

Instead of picking my way through, treating them like the sheep of Texel, I decided to stick to a path behind the grass. There were further shades of Texel as the road carried on and on and on, the one difference being that there was an option of shade this time. Despite slapping on the Factor 50 I could still feel my skin sizzle; the alternative was to head left into overhanging bushes and be bitten. It seemed my lack of spatial awareness had come back to bite me in a more painful way than any bugs in the bushes. Following an hour or so of walking, the bridge looked further away than ever. I wasn't walking to the bridge today, but I spotted a small marina where I thought I might, with steady hands, be able to get some kind of shot of the bridge on full zoom.

Heading across the grass to reach the jetty, there was a cheery wave and nod from a man striding along the path with a newspaper under his arm. It took more seconds than it should have to realise that he was also completely naked. Without meaning to stare I turned and watched him break into an easy jog, glad that I witnessed it from behind.

From behind a high bank of grass another man appeared, also unclothed. The first fellow stopped and they had a conversation.

Erratic wandering had allowed me to blunder on to a naturist beach where people of all ages, shapes, and sizes were enjoying being blanketed by nothing but warm sun. They probably felt my embarrassment – but not as keenly as I did. What was the cool thing to do? What was the right thing to do? There would be no possible scenario in which I joined them. I had made it to the best spot for the shot and had to try it, but taking out my camera I made exaggerated gestures to show that the lens was pointing away from the sunbathers. Then I scrammed. The picture was bloody useless too.

Walking back towards the city, I stopped at a beachside café where everyone was only 90% naked. I went for the ice-cream cone rather than a popsicle. There was such a culture of body confidence here that I headed into town, bought a bikini, and came back. Don't be daft – of course I didn't. I wished I could, but it was thwarted by my woeful level of body confidence after name-calling at school and then being informed in adulthood that my body wasn't acceptable with extra pounds. It seems not everyone loves handles.

So culture called again. At Malmö Castle, where there are several museums including the castle itself, the Malmö Museum interiors were cool in design and temperature. The exhibition called Welcome to Sweden told the stories of people who were housed in the museum when it became a refugee camp for survivors of Nazi concentration camps. These were stories that came back to me again and again during the trip. The crucial bond of the people of Europe.

With my feet in good shape, even in sandals, long walks were providing more than exercise. Even without a map, it wasn't difficult to chance upon lovely squares that were busy with locals sitting enjoying relaxed chats in the sun. Leaving Malmö, I had the distinct impression that there was much more – maybe making that call would have been a good idea.

By this stage there was something of a balance between being prepared and being unprepared enough to let surprises happen. Being completely gormless can mean that even booking accommodation in the wrong town can yield the most glorious results.

The intention was to stop in the hometown of ABBA's Agnetha Fältskog, which is a bit fangirl I know, but I don't care. Getting my köpings mixed up meant that instead of booking in Agnetha's Jönköping, I booked a room in a Norrköping hostel. Thankfully I realised before arriving. Norrköping is a city fighting back from the collapse of industrialisation that has blighted so many working towns across Europe, and a bit like home really.

I had left Malmö and its glorious railway station café three hours before, but even after 6pm it was more than balmy, and getting to the hostel was an uphill task. That's not a metaphor – it was uphill and it was really steep. The plod took me through residential areas, then a small square with a few bars and shops that led on to a bridge. This area was the former industrial heart of the city. Norrköping was known as Sweden's Manchester, with cotton the fabric of the city in this huge network of textile mills.

While Dundee ran on jute rather than cotton, the hulking buildings were familiar, as was the way in which buildings were being reused in imaginative ways.

Separated by the rushing of the Motala, which runs to the Baltic Sea, the mills are connected by steel bridges that create a criss-cross pattern above the water – it is a thing of real beauty against the ochre-painted buildings. These buildings have vast internal spaces that have been used to house everything from cinemas to scientific research centres. Most of these lovely structures were closed for the day, but the hostel was also part of a former mill.

If I could get in. The code e-mailed to me to gain entry to an external door was being rejected noisily by the keypad. Again, there was no-one on the premises, so a call to the number on the door was required to get past the entrance.

It was a private room with shared facilities, but it would appear that the sharing didn't involve too many others. With long institution-like corridors, white walls, and grey floors this was *One Flew Over the Cuckoo's Nest* furnished by IKEA. The reception desk, partially obscured behind shutters, didn't seem to have a drugs cabinet or a record player to soothe us through medication time.

The room itself was minimalist but far from relaxing, even with a ludicrously large TV. The novelty of foreign news programmes and weather forecasts had worn off. It was rolling news, usually CNN and usually involving Donald Trump. Who needs that in their life?

Norrköping was quiet for a comfortable evening stroll to grab some hot food, take it back to the hostel and get some bearings for the next day. The plan was thwarted with the early closing of every takeaway place in this part of town. Supermarket salad it is. The ingredients for a Caesar or a Niçoise salad were always a surprise, but potato was at the top of most lists. The common area was deserted anyway. Eerily so. The corridor became more like *The Shining* than *Cuckoo's Nest* and I was terrified to turn round for fear of encountering scary twins.

The next day's journey to Stockholm would only take an hour or so, leaving the best part of a day here. With nothing covering the windows to block out morning light, I woke early and managed to grab a shower before any of the other residents. They were there. I had heard them laughing, so they were there. Weren't they?

With an agreement that I could leave my bag in the room until after the usual check-out time, I headed out for the day before reception staff had arrived. The coffee shop was surprised that they had a genuine tourist, and a non-Swede at that. I quickly dismissed the notion of telling them that the idea was to walk in Agnetha's footsteps but had got it a bit wrong. I did tell them, cheerily, about the parallels between their city and mine. Blank looks all round. Even mentioning the cake didn't help. I wasn't going to move on to Captain Scott's RRS Discovery and the *Beano* after bringing out the cultural big gun first.

A building I had spotted the night before was the place that could tell the city's back story. Anyone who has visited New York will double take when they catch sight of this, the Museum of Work, which is in a building called The Iron. It's not as flat, but it predates the iconic Fifth Avenue corner building. The Arbetets Museum tells the textile history of Norrköping from the people's point of view, with the stairwells dedicated to the life of one millworker, using not only pictures of her at work but also rounding out her life with family photographs, clothing, and even the suitcase she would take on holiday. The main exhibition spaces are bright and imaginative and transform what could be a dull tale of industrial decline into an inspirational story of how a town got back on its feet.

The top floor is given over to a photography exhibition that provides a more philosophical look at the world of work, including one image of a job centre with Ludo pieces queueing outside. Take that corporate bosses.

It's strange to think that the stairwells and spaces were once full of workers, hurrying to start a shift or weary at the end of a hard day. Now it's visitors, many of whom struggle to climb the stairs after sitting at a desk in front of a screen every day.

Norrköping has extended its regeneration to play as well as work with Knappingsborg, an almost hidden courtyard of artists, independent shops, bars, and restaurants that looked like it could really come alive at night. It was another blunder of research and I wished it had been located the night before. Even though Stockholm was only 90 minutes away, the accommodation was already booked and the train reservation purchased.

Arriving back at the hostel to pick up the backpack it looked like I was back on the beach in Malmö. Sitting at the desk, the receptionist was naked. A man in his 60s perhaps, he wondered why I yelped as he stood up. Fortunately he was only stripped to the waist, complaining that these old buildings were either too hot or too cold. I left before the temperature increased any further.

Arriving in Stockholm was exciting and not just because of ABBA, but quite a lot because of ABBA. When I was 10, the Swedes were at their absolute height. The records, the videos, the film – they were a huge part of my pre-teen world and made a little girl incredibly happy. I was so sure I would win a competition to meet them, run by *Multi-Coloured Swap Shop*, a Saturday morning TV show – that when the tombola turned and my postcard wasn't pulled out, I was devastated.

I still love ABBA – I never stopped loving ABBA. Stockholm was the location I always associated with them and now, on Djurgården island, there was ABBA – The Museum.

That was for later. First it was time to enjoy walking through the city, past the harbour and up to Södermalm where my hotel was situated. It was important that the hotel was close to the port as the next leg would be a ferry to Finland – and it was an early one.

In fact the hotel was so close to the ferry port that I didn't even require a recce to make sure I didn't get lost, but in any case Södermalm turned out to be the best place to stay. From the booking app the hotel looked incredibly stylish, and although it was little more expensive than I would have liked, Stockholm felt like a special occasion.

Wandering through Gamla Stan, the old town, and over towards Södermalm was one of those life-affirming moments. The light, the city, the prospect of spending a few days in this city. It didn't have the instant crush of Copenhagen either. Something about its make-up of islands made it feel open and breathable.

The hotel lived up to its promise, as far as reception. Having booked a room with private facilities I was shown to a basement room with a shared bathroom and a small skylight. The wallpaper had a green forest pattern though, so that helped me breathe.

The receptionist rolled her eyes and told me the manager was *always getting it wrong*. I had four nights here. I had paid for three but the sailing had scuppered me again and another night had been added at the last minute.

There began a game of cat and mouse with the owner to find out how this had happened and what the compensation would be... The mouse won. She never appeared. But the cat came back and refused to pay for the final night. The receptionist shrugged.

The breakfast was great, despite the fact that there was nowhere to eat it apart from reception. With no regard to budget, the receptionists refilled each juice jug with proper freshly squeezed and restocked each muffin basket liberally, encouraging guests to stick as much in their bags as possible.

Stockholm also held the possibility of seeing friends. Although my friend Colin, who works in the city, was away, I found out that Dundee chums were in Stockholm on a family holiday. With an attempt to stay away from Facebook as much as possible, there had been *I'm alive* pictures posted every few days. Following a few messages with Elaine we agreed to get together for an ABBA Museum visit on a day when rain was forecast.

The next day was bright and clear and it seemed Stockholm had a light all of its own. The buildings had been painted in the most exquisite palette, but whether it was the paint or the early morning light, or maybe a combination, they looked like honey and cinnamon and lemon and rose and pistachio and were even more delicious against the pale blue sky.

Gamla Stan was quiet and peaceful with retailers in the narrow streets still setting up for the day. I was beginning the sixth week of the journey and, although I had filled notebooks with thousands of words, it felt like there was nothing concrete.

Conscious that there was a laptop, albeit a creaky one, sitting in London, it looked like I had been typing for so long that I was finding it difficult to turn ideas into words without a keyboard. For the first time, it was time to go shopping. The concern was weight. It had to be light, which meant it would be expensive – and this was Scandinavia – great choice Wilson. However, the next chance to buy something in the rest of Europe would be at least a week away. With two lengthy ferry journeys and long train trips ahead, that was valuable writing time wasted.

It was Sunday in Stockholm and having filled my boots at breakfast (the waist pack had no room for a takeaway) I was fuelled and ready to go. With the laptop purchased and safely back in my dungeon I plugged it in to charge and decided to work out the Swedish keyboard later. There was no story in the purchase. I asked a handsome young man to show me the lightest laptop and he sold it to me. The price was better than expected but it's hardly an anecdote.

It was afternoon in Gamla Stan now. The streets were busier with souvenir shops open and doing great business. Even the racks of postcards, flags, and plastic Viking helmets couldn't cheapen the charm of the place though. Having no need for a helmet with pigtails (want and need aren't the same thing) I explored the side streets where many bars were happy to offer sanctuary over an expertly chilled local cider.

It was a fantastically aimless day that later took me for what can only be described as an amble around the harbour, eating an open sandwich with perfect smoked salmon, drinking white wine, and feeling ridiculous excitement every time the number 7 tram passed. This was the one that travelled right to the front door of ABBA – The Museum and was decorated with huge photographs of them in their heyday.

Monday brought the predicted downpour, so I spent the morning getting to grips with the laptop before heading to the museum via a short ferry ride. Stew and I, friends since secondary school, had been in a band together so I knew this would be up his street, but Elaine appeared even keener. Their boys – less so.

The rain was cascading from awnings when we met outside the museum, with Elaine confessing that Aidan had protested that morning that ABBA were the worst thing to ever happen to humanity. I could understand that the museum being next to the Gröna Lund amusement park must really have rubbed salt into the boys' wounds.

For me, this was every theme park rolled into one. The journey of ABBA from their early days, to playing in the folk parks individually, to their meeting, to Eurovision, and right through the years of making glorious music, to the end (sniff). The boys brightened at the interactive shenanigans where they could create avatars, and a re-creation of the recording studio with the original mixing desk was enough for musician Stew.

The rainy day meant it was crowded but it didn't take away from the absolute joy of the experience. With a promise to the boys that they would be visiting the amusement park on a dry day, we spent a relaxing day of cider and chat and ended up sitting outside a bar in Södermalm on what was now a dry and slightly balmy evening. It was a tram and a bus back to their holiday home, but a gentle weave after a marvellous day back to the hotel for me.

Knowing that the hotel had no set breakfast times, there was a possibility of a little lie-in to let the slight hangover settle. The young woman on reception would keep replenishing stocks until they ran out it seemed.

It's difficult to escape water in Stockholm, and why would anyone want to? On a wander along Strandvägen on the north side of the small bay at Nybroviken, I chanced upon the footbridge access to Djurgården. The Museum of Nordic Life seemed a good option, particularly as it was a life I was hankering after. Again there were no foosty (Scottish word again, for musty, but foosty is better) cabinets with tiny shards of pottery here.

There were more chairs of course, but also inspiring room sets and a gallery that explored universal experiences, from birth to death and all inbetween, all illustrated with stories from real life.

Having given the Absolut vodka museum a swerve, and not even contemplating Gröna Lund following the Tivoli Gardens melancholy, it was tempting to check how late the ABBA museum opened. Don't judge me. The previous day was the fun day. This was serious scholarly study with the audio tour, stopping to read every information board, listening to every piece of additional audio, watching everything the cinema had to offer, and hanging around the studio for far too long. The piano is hooked up to Benny's home studio and when he starts playing there the museum piano will play the same... It didn't. Ah well. It was early evening on this sunny day and while the museum wasn't exactly empty, there was minimal external noise and buzz. Nothing to distract an Abbanorak.

With the early morning start, there was time for one last wander around Gamla Stan and Södermalm before heading back to the hotel to pack and set the alarm. The sailing was 7.45pm but check in was 90 minutes earlier and I had to find the place, which I still wasn't taking for granted. The map app said take the first left, walk 15 minutes, then turn right – it hadn't met me though.

The last sight of the receptionist was not insisting that I pay my final night's bill, but while she set out an elaborate buffet with wine and told me to help myself. Her other guests seemed to be distinctly of the non-resident variety.

I'd give you the name, but we have to presume it won't be in business much longer.

It's all the same
if it rains or not.

Kimi Raikonnen

TERMINALEN STADSGÅRDEN hadn't even opened its doors. So concerned that I would be walking the wrong way up a dual carriageway as the ferry disappeared beyond the horizon, I arrived half an hour before the staff. It had been raining overnight, however, and the streets had that freshly washed scent. I had a sense of feeling truly alive – something that had been happening at the most unexpected junctures. There was no sunrise as such but a heavenly morning light. Stockholm will always mean light to me. And ABBA.

A daytime sailing meant that there were no worries about cabins and having to avoid snoring, snuffling strangers. It did mean having to fill the next 12 hours, but the laptop would help. Reading hadn't worked so far, particularly in public. You need to travel alone to realise how noisy the world can be. The clouds of chatter can be distracting enough in English, but try to concentrate when surrounded by the lyrical rhythms of another language.

The weather turned nasty as we departed Stockholm, with the tallest rides at Gröna Lund shrouded in mist and the city disappearing under thick cloud. The ferry was shiny and modern and some passengers had found their method of passing the 12 hours already – the bars were open. The smaller passengers began the day exercising their lungs and decided that they liked it. For the longest time it felt that we weren't at sea. Even beyond the Stockholm archipelago there are endless islands and completely open sea was rare. There was nowhere to hide. Nowhere that was quiet anyway. Every possible inch of space is given over to selling. Food in the never-ending restaurants and buffets, alcohol in too many bars and in those bars entertainment from bands of varying sizes and abilities. Watching a covers band in the largest lounge, it was easy to see how they were feeling behind the fixed smiles. The six-piece were working it, despite playing to 11 people in the cavernous nightclub, watching one couple waltz (they weren't playing a waltz) and three children hitting one another with balloons. Living the dream.

From a blast of soft rock to the constant rattle and ping of amusement arcades, to the bustle and melting plastic of Duty Free, I somehow managed to wander the decks for several hours, stopping only to buy a coffee and a slice of bizarre Swiss Roll.

On a dry day, I could have escaped on deck. When the rain eased from torrential to simply lashing, I would put my back into getting the door open to the outside and hold on to my hat, my glasses, my life… It wasn't pleasant. It wasn't even quiet.

Finally managing to locate an empty seat away from anything that would necessitate spending money, people watching took an interesting turn. I had spotted a woman earlier with what I presumed was unusual dress sense. A long velvet skirt with an elaborate bustle and sequinned apron was partnered with a high-necked blouse complete with ruffles and puffed sleeves. Her long hair was in ribbons. Fair enough, I wasn't the picture of elegance myself. Now she approached again, accompanied by at least six other women who were all dressed in a similar way. There were men alongside, dressed simply in dark trousers, plain shirts, and jackets.

With a little internet research it transpired that these were Finnish Kale, a branch of the Romany people who moved into Finland and Sweden after migrating from Scotland and England in the 16th century. The Kale woman maintained the long skirts, aprons, and blouses – traditional dress for Finnish women – long after their non-Kale counterparts abandoned them for modern dress. Then in great Gypsy tradition they decided to bling it up, making it as shiny and elaborate as possible.

Passengers began to split into distinct categories. The mature couple, affluent and sophisticated, and probably with an expensive Volvo in the car deck topped with canoes and bicycles; families with young children, generally found in the café or one of the play areas provided; and bikers, lots of bikers. There appeared to be fellow solo travellers, but we were all beyond help. With eyes that said, *will this never end?* we could be spotted in corners, praying for land.

There was a flurry of excitement when the ferry made a stop at Marienhamn, the capital of Åland, an independent island that has its own government but is still under Finnish sovereignty. From there until the port of Turku, there was no open sea, just the hulking ferry rounding the islands that lie off the coast of Finland.

Once on the ground in Turku, the fear was having to find my way as I did in Hirtshals, only in heavy rain. This time I was heading straight to a hotel, however, and even a walk of 45 minutes in stormy conditions seemed like the ultimate freedom.

I had bought a fancy designer rain poncho in Aarhus, but this was its first real workout. It covered the backpack too, so reflections in windows revealed that I resembled a self-delivering damask sofa. The streets were empty, apart from this floating brown and black sofa. And when a fire engine passed with sirens blaring, proper European sirens mind, I thought, jeez wouldn't it be funny if…?

It wasn't funny. Even a few hundred metres from my hotel it was clear that guests had congregated outside on the pavement as firefighters investigated. Once they had emerged, it was safe to go in. Entry was by keycode again, but no sooner had I got into my room, the TV sprung to life and an overhead announcement began. Both told me it was time to vamoose, there was a fire. The nearest exit – you know the drill. So I did, I hadn't even put my backpack down so there was no rule that I had to leave it. I was the only person at my nearest exit, a pitch black spiral staircase from the fourth floor. Finding my way back outside involved passing through various rooms, including one that looked like the engine room of the Titanic, and emerging in a street I didn't recognise. This was the rear of the building and once I had found my way to the front the firefighters were shrugging and reassuring me – and only me – that all was cool. No-one else had evacuated.

Back in the room I could appreciate the Soviet spy chic of it all. Again it was booked for cost and location, but this room was massive with a seating area, kitchen, and generous bed. If a surface wasn't covered in dark wood veneer it was wrapped in a bright red synthetic fabric rarely seen outside of fire safety films – as the stuff that goes up. Apart from a small kitchen area there was a hefty supply of take-out menus. With my belly reminding me that a slice of luminous Swiss Roll really wasn't enough for the day, I headed to the nearest source of hot food, a pizza place in the next block.

It was almost 10pm, so pizza in front of the telly while a thunderstorm brewed outside didn't seem like too much of an indulgence. The pizza was excellent and I settled on *The Bridge*, in Danish and Swedish, but with Finnish subtitles.

Apart from Turku being the place where the ferry landed from Sweden, I knew little else. The next day I found that the thunderstorm had used its huge broom and swept the terrible weather away, leaving a comfortably sunny day behind. The night before had been about getting to the hotel and nothing else. This was the first chance to see Turku properly, and it was good.

It was apparent that the Russian influences didn't end with the hotel room decor. Turku had the same multi-hued charm of buildings in Stockholm, with an occasional splash of Art Nouveau, but there were also hulking brutes of buildings that pointed to several periods of Russian occupation. It had been the capital of Finland until 1812, but those occupiers decided it was too close to Sweden and moved the capital further east to Helsinki. This was all news to me. The city that revealed itself was simply extremely cool.

As the trip continued, my fitness levels were steadily increasing and, except for days with sailings or long train journeys, four hours of walking was the minimum. Turku kept me moving, keen to cover as much ground as possible. It was market day, the square packed with stalls selling fresh fruit and vegetables. In the corner was an old tram car that had been converted into an ice-cream parlour. There was a take-away window but also the chance to sit on high stools and soak in the atmosphere of not only the tram car but also the square itself. Serving was a future Miss Finland, working between the busy window and the seating area effortlessly.

On the south bank of the River Aura that runs through the city, it was time to break that self-imposed rule of avoiding churches. The heavens had opened and Turku Cathedral was the only place of sanctuary. It was clear that others had the same idea and once the rain stopped the heathens scarpered. At least I had the good grace to go to the café below and buy coffee and cake, which at five Euros for a spoonful of coffee, some hot water, and a miniscule fruit pie, had gone to the top of the rip-off list.

It was more expensive than the entrance to the Sibelius museum, where a central concert hall is surrounded by an exhibition charting not only the composer's life, but also the history of musical instruments in the area. Knowing that visitors can have itchy fingers there's a harpsichord to satisfy the desire to play. But that day it was me and the man on reception. Apart from that, silence. The last thing needed was my ham-fisted attempts to strangle a tune from a harpsichord.

Even this small stretch to the south of the river showed why Turku had been a European Capital of Culture in 2011. The thought of archaeological excavation and ruins in general provokes little more than a yawn from me usually, but here at Aboa Vetus there is an underground city that, while not intact of course, shows clearly what the medieval city was like. This is the excavated Convent Quarter, with ruins of stone houses, streets, and stairways. Archaeologists are still excavating and that everyday work is part of the exhibition. Head lamps switched off, they will stop to answer questions. I have no idea what they said – it was in Finnish, or maybe Swedish – the city is bilingual. The other half of the building is the contemporary art gallery Ars Nova, with modern art that didn't infuriate.

There was one more destination here before heading back across – the Handicrafts Museum at Luostarinmäki. I know it sounds uncool and a bit knitted lentil casserole. At first it had the look of Den Gamle By in Aarhus. The difference is that the wooden village here is completely original; an entire district that survived a massive fire in 1827 due to its location on the outskirts of the city, the only place artists and craftsmen could afford to live. When modern health and safety concerns took over the artists had to move out and the city took over to preserve the district as an open-air museum. The artists and craftsmen are back, but part-time, with open workshops where they can demonstrate and sell work. This isn't a recent idea, however, it opened in 1940. Peeking through courtyards and climbing rickety wooden staircases, visitors can see artists wearing period costume. This isn't over-the-top living history – and the artists are remarkably tolerant of some ridiculous questions.

In the workshop of a printer, a rotund chap in a pale blue smock and small peaked cap inked the press and pulled the heavy lever. When I caught his eye and said thank you, he handed me the postcard he had just taken off the press. A souvenir in the correct sense of the word. It was a black and white line cut drawing of Turku Castle.

The Aura is narrow but this allows to the city to feel more connected. A free ferry, the Föri, runs back and forth continuously for pedestrians and cyclists. It took 90 seconds to get to the north bank. Yes, there were bridges closer, but who wouldn't make the effort to take a 90-second ferry trip. Heading along the banks of the river, a sculpture of a giant daisy appeared. The day couldn't get any brighter.

With no idea where the hell the train station was, it seemed wise to locate it for the next day's two-hour journey to Helsinki. The route took me through residential areas and, for once, there was a serious consideration of what kind of life I could live in Turku. The back streets were filled with shops that might have been original, might have been retro, it was difficult to tell.

Choosing a café for a sandwich and coffee, the retro was real. The rye bread roll was on par with the brick I had bought in Hamburg. Choosing it from a chiller cabinet, on examination there was cheese in there, of that I was sure, and the red hinted at tomato. It wasn't so clear that there was also a cold fried egg in there, no butter but a layer of something similar to cottage cheese, and a single strand of lettuce. Even the cup was straight from the set of a 1970s Mike Leigh play. Abigail would have served coffee in these to her party guests.

The problem tooth was becoming increasingly difficult to reattach with fixative and there was no way that it would survive this onslaught. With a slight tug it was out and snuggled down in a safe place in the waist pack, much to the obvious delight of two elderly ladies who had been watching me carefully. As each level of contrasting roll filling assaulted my tastebuds, I reminded myself that this was going native. This wasn't the easy route. Or the edible one. The evening was fine and relaxed and joyous. Even though there were couples and groups enjoying beers together, there was no sadness or regret at being alone here. It was all about Turku – not me.

There was another ferry to book, to travel from Helsinki back into northern Germany. I hoped to get to Helsinki later the following day, giving a little more time in Turku then spend three nights in the capital before catching the ferry, which left at 5pm.

I had spent a fortune on accommodation in Helsinki accidentally. Don't ask how (and there was only one beer involved) but I had somehow mistaken the price for one night as the price for three nights. If it looks too good to be true, it probably is. Receiving an e-mail to ask when I would arrive, I responded to say 4pm, their normal check-in time. It was a studio apartment close to the station and in an achingly contemporary block. At least it was clear where the money was going – and that was even more than before now that a problem with the ferry had added another night in Helsinki.

Arriving at the check-in office, it was empty. The whole place was glass, it was easy to tell. Calling the number on the door and reminding them that THEY had asked ME when I would be there, the voice on the end ignored my dose of the grumps and said cheerily that her colleague would be there soon. It was obvious why he was late – the angels couldn't bear to let him go.

We'll call him Ossi, because that's his name. Tall, but not too tall; tanned, but in that healthy outdoors way; blonde, but not too blonde. He apologised for being late and smiled. I melted and muttered, probably something about it being my fault. I think I might have tossed my hair. He showed me round the incredible studio apartment with balcony – one that was costing me the equivalent of a month's rent at home for four nights. Even the quirky Finnish way to turn on the dishwasher was fascinating. Everything was promptly lost in a haze of… so, are his eyes blue or grey?

As we parted and he gently shook me off his ankle, he said that if there were any problems I should call. I immediately looked for problems but there were none. This place was perfect. So perfect, in fact, that it was time to play house. It's strange how the most mundane household chores can seem enjoyable after a few weeks off. With a washing machine and dryer, a full laundry could take me into the next stage of the journey and this sparkling kitchen could be the answer to saving some money on meals.

At the supermarket 10 minutes' away, I unhooked a small trolley and shopped for four days of meals. It took three hours. It was fascinating. It took 20 minutes to browse the liquorice aisle and pick a few bags to send home to a liquorice-loving friend. With groceries unpacked, there was still time to have a bit of a dander around the city centre area. It was Friday night and there was time for a quiet beer before heading back to my bachelorette apartment.

Being so close to the centre, I was thrown straight into a busy Helsinki Saturday. Having exited the station from the side, I hadn't seen the bold frontage of Helsinki station, which it seems is in the national romanticist style. Whatever it is, it takes a good few minutes to soak it in. If anything, it showed again how Finland differs from its Scandinavian neighbours. It showed how much it had in common with the Baltic states. With a ferry to Tallinn in Estonia taking less than two hours, the architecture showed Finland as the point where Scandi and Baltic meets as Nordic.

In the cathedral square the sides were lined by tour buses, straight from the cruises and hop-on hop-off sightseeing buses. The city harbour area was lively, with a market selling everything from original art to hand-knitted hats in a range of animals, to a lunch of salmon soup and rustic bread. There were some gorgeous hats. Not the animals, but others that were perfect for the sun as well as stylish. The lucky sunhat was perched on my head, loyal and still perfectly acceptable after lasting longer than a marriage and a long-term relationship. I felt disloyal, but the stallholder told me that she would only be there for another hour. She could smell a sale; I could smell bullshit. I walked away, wishing I hadn't had such a hefty breakfast at the apartment. That soup smelled good.

It was Saturday and at the Uspenski Orthodox Cathedral a young bride was entering with her father. A couple of cruise passengers went to follow (they had their name badges on) and when told that it was closed to visitors because of the wedding, they raged that they were only there for the day! They pointed out that they were the kind of people that spent money in this city and they should be treated better than this – then repeated that this was their only day in Helsinki. The gentleman at the door waited for them to finish and with a calm demeanour pointed out in flawless English that the young couple getting married had spent their whole lives in Helsinki – and this was the only day they would be getting married.

I had a tentative plan to head to a sauna for a massage. The legs and feet were in good shape but the muscles could probably do with some attention. And even though the backpack was comparatively light there was still some strain on my shoulders. When it came to entering the sauna, however, I just couldn't do it. Even though the sandals were back on, my body self-consciousness was still crippling at times.

No matter, the harbour was a great place to soak up the weekend. Heading back into the city, a large crowd had gathered to drink beer and whoop at an outdoor concert in a square. The band were great and the lead singer performed as if he was trying to communicate with punters at the back of an enormodome. Even better.

With no great desire to visit too many museums or galleries, I decided to take a day off and spend the whole of the next day in the swish apartment I was paying so much for. It was wise. There were threatening early morning black clouds, and they followed through on that threat. It was a chance to look through my clothing, now a little worse for wear from numerous sink washes. Here they could get a decent wash and maybe even an iron. That's how much I was craving domesticity.

It was also a chance to plan ahead a little. The next few countries shouldn't prove too much of a challenge, but Eastern Europe wasn't too far away.

It felt like a long day after having been so active. I still couldn't concentrate to read and a few hours of writing felt like enough for a sleepy Sunday. Sleepy until my German neighbours came back from what must have been a Sunday session and started playing loud music and crushing my Zen. They were on the adjoining balcony so maybe a few withering looks across the fence would help.

Now, minimalism is fantastic and natural light is my favourite of all the lights, but when you forget that there's a wall of glass between you and said balcony it's easy to walk straight into it. It's a strange thing. The shock is worse than the pain, and then the lurching stomach when you eventually locate the spectacles that have landed across the room with one leg pointing the wrong way. The tooth went flying too.

First things first. I wouldn't find the tooth without the spectacles. I tentatively placed them on my face, with the twisted leg nowhere near its usual resting place. Terrified to touch it lest it snap completely, I tilted my head to the side to locate the tooth.

Hey. Great idea. Call Ossi to tell him about my neighbours from Hell. With my wonky tooth and broken specs. He'd no doubt be off cooking a romantic dinner for a Finnish model. I'd get the duty manager who would tell me to grow up and have some fun.

First thing Monday and the great optician search didn't last long. She took them away for five minutes and brought them back almost as good as new and there was no charge. One pair of clip-on sunshades and two cleaning cloths later, they had 40 Euros from me anyway. After a day with no exercise at all, a long walk up to the Olympic Stadium felt good. This is retro Olympics, a stadium and tall tower from the 1952 games. Access was limited due to a gymnastics thing but it was possible to go up to the top of the tower, by lift, for five Euros. At first I muttered about being perfectly capable of using stairs, but they were out of bounds. Once I reached the top and spotted some balustrades held together with bright orange tape, I was glad to use the zippy lift. There was a good old view over the city, but these high up adventures don't really do much for me. I'd much rather be at ground level looking up.

The clip-on sunglasses weren't required, with the day veering from overcast to splodges of rain. The poncho was handy but as soon as it went on the rain stopped, as soon as it was folded back in its own pouch – devilishy clever design – the rain began again. With a hot lunch over, it looked like an indoors afternoon with the Finnish Design Museum challenging the Danish in its bounty of beauty – even without Mr Jacobsen. The Finnish experience had been truly wonderful. Unexpected self-assurance in what it had to offer and people who were generally friendly, welcoming, and bloody gorgeous.

It was time to check out and say farewell to the awesome Ossi. When he asked if I was travelling back to Scotland, I gave him a brief explanation of the trip. He seemed impressed. Oh yeah baby. He was impressed. E-mail addresses exchanged and everything.

It was time to find the Helsinki Metro. The port and my passage back to northern Germany was a little out of the city. The sailing was at 5pm so of course I started my journey at midday. It was a simple journey. Take the Metro to Vuosaari, then a bus to the port. I left the train at the correct station and walked into a deserted housing estate, wandering through a maze of walk-ups and apartment blocks but saw no-one to ask. Muttering under my breath about transport websites making it look like it was easy, it turned out to be, well, easy. If I had turned right rather than left to exit I would have walked straight into the station.

There was more than enough time, however, even for my warped sense of direction. I even had time to let a bus go past and take a photo of some particularly bad swear words for friends back home. They loved it, which made falling backwards into some shrubbery worthwhile.

On the next bus, it was worth double-checking whether it went to the port. The driver took out his earphones, broadcasting the death metal that must accompany his daily routine through the Helsinki suburbs. He nodded and pointed to the display that said three Euros. I handed over the money, took the ticket, and by the time I looked up again he had his earphones in again. He removed them to enquire *Ship?* I nodded and the deal was done. I was the only remaining soul when we reached the Hansa terminal. There was nothing there and, with a couple of hours to kill before check-in opened, the recommendation was to try the lunch restaurant in the next building.

At sea, I learned how little
a person needs, not how much.

Robin Lee Graham, *sailor*

THE LUNCH WAS never-ending, with each subsequent course a case of passing the time rather than satisfying hunger. I knew I had the right to be there, but it felt like stumbling into a subsidised workplace canteen – that certain ambience of wilting lettuce and tiny soup bowls with handles. There are charming moments everywhere, however, and to watch four suited and booted businessmen serve themselves from large tubs of ice-cream, taking a wee bit more of this and a wee bit more of that and then a few sprinkles, showed the humanity behind the posturing and the big talk – not that I could understand a word they were saying.

The sailing was 28 hours so thank goodness a cabin was affordable. At least there would be an escape from the constant noise. Unlike the slick embarcation for foot passengers elsewhere, the few of us who weren't in cars had to be taken on board by mini-bus before any other vehicles.

That crucial first exploration was… well, it was shorter than usual. There was a buffet restaurant and a bar that doubled as a café. There was a small children's play area. Apart from that we were doomed to be zombies on the high seas, wandering the teak-panelled halls of this Scooby Doo ghost ship of the Baltic. That's not true actually, there was a small lounge where it was quiet enough to read, but also quiet enough that bikers felt they could take off their boots and subject us to the multi-sensory assault of their socks and snoring. And there was a sauna, but let's not go there – of course I didn't.

The Swedish showbands and Danish bingo and Norwegian drunkards were looking pretty good now.

The cabin itself was hardly *Love Boat* glamour either, with the same particular shade of brown on the walls and the floor and the ceiling. Once at sea, however, the weather was absolutely glorious. Blue skies and calm seas meant that sitting on deck for a while was possible. Looking over the top deck to the rear of the ship, the real purpose of this ship was evident. Cargo.

For too many hours I drifted between the top deck and the cabin, each becoming more charmless as the hours wore on. Wine helped. A windowless cabin meant that there was no way to tell if it was night or day and there was no reason to get up early the next morning, apart from more of the same until reaching Travemünde at 9.30pm. Save for a range of what can only be described as zany European game shows, the cabin TV had the equivalent of a flight tracker, showing where we were in the Baltic, but to a soundtrack that went beyond creepy. There was little to do but try to focus on anything apart from the open sea and watching the clock. The silence of this cruise was almost as distracting as the constant noise of the others.

Arriving so late meant an overnight stay in Lübeck before a marathon travelling day. The Travemünde destination was generally written as Lübeck/ Travemünde, leading the witless traveller into a false sense of security that they were the same thing. We were driven off the boat again, this time by an extremely jolly German. It was 10.30pm by now and outside the terminal was darkness – a surprise after after the long Nordic nights. There was one taxi, which I let the other foot passengers take as they had a small grumpy boy in tow. Ferry workers said that there probably wouldn't be any others as foot passengers are rare on this route. A bus it was, from one of several stops, and an hour later I was on a bus that the driver didn't say wasn't going to Lübeck, so that was good enough for me.

The brief side trip from Hamburg paid off. Recognising the landmarks and main streets meant that I arrived at the youth hostel not too long after midnight. I wanted to pay, fall into a bunk, and have a deep sleep before heading off in the morning.

An hour later I had the key to a room. Part of the booking meant I had to join the Jugendhergerbe Association, the German Youth Hostelling Association, and be given a full and detailed explanation of the benefits and how the card could be used internationally. The young chap was so enthusiastic that I couldn't break his flow and make him aware that I wasn't really a hosteller and I certainly wasn't a youth. This was probably a one-time deal.

From Lübeck, smooth changes at Hamburg and Basel meant that even though the train left at 9am, I was in Bern by 6pm. The streets were familiar from a long time ago. On the Swiss school trip, the one that had taken us on the ferry, then through Germany and on to Switzerland, Bern had been one of the day trips. Although my lasting memory of the city is the shock at hearing the price of a bar of chocolate, these streets and landmarks like the

Zytglogge clock tower were familiar. This time Bern would be my base for a few days, with side trips to locations where any remaining suitable accommodations had price tags I couldn't justify. The backpacker hostel was basic but in a central location and had private rooms. It also had teeny tiny staircases, which were fine for me but not for the two Japanese girls who arrived behind me. Their suitcases were huge and shiny and clearly weighed more than they did, but the swivelling wheels were no help in negotiating the stairs. One of them actually cried. Helping her up the final flight I couldn't help asking, *What the hell have you got in there?* The answer being, *Not so much.*

Reception was supposed to be open from 3 to 10pm, but at 7pm was closed. When the beautifully illustrated lady returned half an hour later, she was taken aback that there should be people in reception. The girls clapped in glee when they saw I was accessing my room on the fifth floor by lift, until they realised that theirs was in another part of the building. Throwing the room window open for any kind of breeze, I saw it overlooked the red-tiled roofs and a street where people of all ages were relaxing with early evening beers, but hanging too far out of the window could mean hitting the cobbles below. The evening still had a fierce heat to it so I switched on the fan and let it push the toasty air around.

The arcades and squares were busy as the sun began to go down, but there was still time to have a proper tourist dinner at a restaurant on Baren-platz. By now, any thoughts of eating alone had shifted from the alone to the eating. The sizzling skillet that arrived was potatoes and cheese, nothing more than that and all the better for it. Cheese had already become a staple in the travelling diet as had beer, so why not eh? The large mug of Gurten was the perfect partner. And now that we were in central Europe, beer came in glasses with a sturdy handle. Diners around me were a mix of locals and visitors; the locals appeared to be academics. They were certainly discussing interesting things, a conversation that on any other night I would have been delighted to join. Tonight was all about the tatties and cheese and beer and sun and planning the next day's adventure.

There was a bit of a delay that morning. The receptionist looked expectantly as I wandered past and asked if I would be checking out now. Our paperwork didn't match. Someone else was booked into my room that night and there was nothing else free. I hadn't checked the amount and only one night had come off even if my confirmation said I had three nights. There was a bit of a panic to get a room that lay somewhere between that 12-bed dorm nightmare and five-star bankruptcy. Packing, booking, and chastising myself that I hadn't double-checked the booking the night before, it wasn't the start to the day I had planned, but it was becoming pretty clear that shit happened and dealing with it was the key. With the backpack deposited just 10 minutes and an extra 50 Euros a night away, it was time to skip further down memory lane. The school trip had taken us to Interlaken, a town that was around an hour away. My original plan was to stay there, but all that remained were extremely basic hostels for the extreme sports dudes who flocked to the area. I didn't investigate the luxury end. The hotel we had stayed in all those years ago didn't appear to be operating – probably eaten by ants if the previous stay was anything to go by.

On a clear summer's day, the journey was more than spectacular with water in the glacial lakes mirroring the hue of the sky. There was barely a straight stretch of track as the train rounded the lakes and carved its way through the mountains. The station at Interlaken Ost was the gateway to shops selling expensive Swiss watches, expensive handbags, and anything expensive really. It was tour group central with many taking advantage of tax-free status to take home some swag, then heading to the casino set back from the Höheweg.

Nothing was familiar – absolutely nothing. Not even the massive great mountains. Then again, at 13 years old most people are more occupied by laughing with their friends and wondering if people are snogging than the architecture or majesty of the landscape. There were souvenir shops of course, but not quite as many selling hats with feathers or cuckoo clocks as I remember. Posters promoted trips up the Schilthorn in cable cars, prompting flashbacks to being almost 3000m up at the top of that mountain as well the trip to Bern. My only crystal-clear memory of Interlaken was someone in the group managing to buy beer, a few of us getting caught, and the teachers' threats that we would be sent home – until they realised that one of the teachers, requiring some assistance to make her way up the stairs, wasn't a great role model for her young charges.

The clear mountain air would obviously have done us good, but what people were wearing and what was on then hotel jukebox were our priorities. The most played song on the jukebox was the number 1 single in the UK at the time, a slice of electro-pop called *Funky Town* by Lipps Inc. And now, at a stall on Höheweg manned by an elderly couple sitting quietly behind their eclectic selection of goods, was a box of seven-inch singles and at the front, *Funky Town* by Lipps Inc.

The decision to take a day trip was a good one. It was clear that Interlaken could be explored in that time, and that was with breaks for refreshments and even a bit of shopping. It was clear that some items of clothing had served their purpose when the laundry was done in Helsinki, so several new T-shirts were required. There were a few real people shops and that most welcome of signs – SALE. Along the stretch there were some interesting retailers, including one that proclaimed it was the last sex shop before the Jungfrau.

It had been a strangely emotional day, throwing up some long-forgotten memories. The weather had shifted from bright sun to pouring rain to a full-on storm that rumbled through the mountains with added bass, and bringing lightning that illuminated the highest peaks. Watching from the safety of a café and being comforted by apple strudel, it was completely exhilarating.

Back in Bern, it was the proving to be a great evening destination, strolling the arcades with a feeling of safety, contentment, and never getting lost.

I am not going to be a star.
I am going to be a legend.

Freddie Mercury

THE NEXT DAY was about music. The Montreux Jazz Festival began that day, but that wasn't the main reason for travelling 90 minutes to that town. It was another kind of *Jazz* that attracted me, it being the title of the first album Queen recorded at Mountains Studio there.

Lake Montreux is where the smoke really was on the water. In December 1971 fire broke out during a concert by Frank Zappa at the lakeside casino. Deep Purple were recording in the town at the time and immortalised the event, inspiring a million bedroom guitarists with that riff, and sending just as many guitar teachers off their rockers.

It was time to visit Freddie Mercury, his statue anyway, a three-metre high bronze placed by the lake in 1996, five years after his death. He spent the bulk of his final years here, recording and living quietly away from the press attention that he would attract in London. Now his statue stops visitors in their tracks, some even leaving flowers.

It wasn't just Freddie of course. Montreux was as elegant as expected and it was clear that the jazz festival had attracted crowds. There was a market stretching along the shore of the lake with music blasting from every stall. It's no exaggeration to say that I winced hearing Vanilla Ice's *Ice Ice Baby*, with its sample from *Under Pressure* by Queen and David Bowie, which had been recorded right here. No respect...

Past the stalls, an arm pierced the blue sky and the full-length Freddie appeared, surrounded by people. Most stopped and had their picture taken with the statue, many striking a classic Mercury stance, but one man was clearly frustrated that he couldn't get a clear shot. When the crowds cleared a little, he was fussing with his expensive-looking camera gear. As I circled to see the statue from every angle, I was the only obstruction to his clear coast. He grunted loudly and motioned at me to move away. Not the most polite approach, but when his path was clear he flicked a timer switch and ran to the base of the statue, smiling at the camera and forming the shape of a heart with his hands around his own heart.

The plaque on the statue's base said that the Mountains Studio was open to visit as part of Queen – The Studio Experience. It wasn't the easiest to find, and the back of a casino complex isn't the most inspiring location. At one point this was all studio. Where people stood below, playing slot machines and throwing their money away, was the main studio floor, where *Don't Stop Me Now* had been recorded. The exhibition is free to enter but visitors are encouraged to make a donation to the Mercury Phoenix Trust that fights AIDS by funding organisations and research worldwide. It's a small exhibition, with the control room still containing the original desk with a few faders exposed to let visitors remix a few Queen tracks. This was the studio where *Under Pressure* was recorded; where David Bowie came down from his home in the town to visit the band and ended up recording that single. A plaque on the floor marks the spot where Freddie recorded his last-ever vocal, *Mother Love*.

These were my art galleries. Where some people flocked to see Picassos, I was more interested in Bjorn's guitar from that fateful Eurovision-winning night, or seeing that Freddie used an SM58 microphone, the very same that I had used in my last band. Here was Freddie's in a presentation case – the one he had crashed his gnashers against for many years on stage. This was part of the Queen memorabilia including costumes, videos, and a recreation of their studio set-up. The outfits included the diaphanous white stage gear that Freddie and Brian May wore in the mid 70s and the harlequin costumes that Freddie favoured in later years.

It was a fascinating place to wander, particularly with no interruptions, until I was joined by my friend from the Freddie statue. He glowered and began to set up the self-timer again. Maybe it was the surroundings and taking on some of Freddie's playful cheek, but for his first few shots I timed it perfectly to walk right into shot. Shoo *me* away will you? When he reached the harlequin costume, I left him alone and watched him rush to the case, strike a full Freddie pose and try to fight back tears. I felt bad at the sabotage; this was clearly his musical pilgrimage. Never judge.

After depositing a donation in the box on the way out, someone who worked at the exhibition appeared and handed me a T-shirt. I suggested that he give it to the superfan inside but he said there was another for him.

A walk up to the old town led back down quite naturally to the buzz of the lakeside and a piano player cranking out the Great American Songbook for passing music fans. When he launched into *Bohemian Rhapsody*, however, it turned into an impromptu singalong. Before joining in I remembered the precarious position of the tooth. He finished to massive applause and a much fuller tip jar.

The journey back to Bern from Montreux was as spectacular as the Interlaken line, until the guy opposite took his shoes off and put his bare feet on the seat beside me. He motioned to say *Do you mind?* Yes I did, I hated it, but what do you say? So, I just gave my most agreeable shrug and watched as he pulled out a plastic bag full of scratch cards. He worked his way through them, sighing at every thwarted fortune. The inspector, I thought, the inspector will shoo those trotters away from my personal space. But no. It seemed the lovely Swiss liked things on time, but shared none of the British displeasure at feet being on seats.

The final few hours in Bern were spent between the rigours of the post office and a bar to recover from the stress. In the German-speaking part of the country, I really thought that I would be fine to communicate, and if not then English would be a certainty. The tiny assistant spoke no English and seemed to think my German was a Martian dialect. We managed to meet in the middle with some French. It took far too long and the package never arrived.

With one more meander around the town at night before darkness had hidden the contrast between the blue waters and red roofs, it struck me how lucky I had been as a child. The beauty and excitement of travel must have been embraced then, even if snogging and jeans and chocolate were the priorities at the time. At times they are still priorities - who wants to grow up that much?

This means nothing
to me either actually...

Any resemblance to a song about Austria is entirely coincidental.

THE NEXT DAY'S journey to Innsbruck was five hours long and, since there was a change at Zurich, it made sense to leave the station, have a look and catch a later train. Great idea, as long as the change was at Hauptbahnhof. This clearly wasn't. I wandered some anonymous back streets for 20 minutes before realising that something was skewed geographically. No more time could be wasted righting this wrong so I checked the app to see whether there was an earlier train to Innsbruck than planned. Zurich would need to wait.

The train was remarkably shoogly and wheezy. The Wi-Fi was free and zippy and stable, but trying to do anything that involved a screen made me nauseated. The train rolled and juddered and gave huge asthmatic gasps for air as it rumbled through countryside that might not give this train journey any special status but it is scenic – incredibly so. The Austrian mountainsides were dotted with proper wooden cabins and this was one journey where I was only too happy to abandon all technology and enjoy. Making choices about the next destination on the hoof was freeing but it also meant that planning was always at the back of my mind. Times when it was possible to let everything go and just be were pretty rare.

Innsbruck was quiet. Strangely quiet. In the bowl of the mountains the silence of the Sunday streets was deafening. By now there were no real surprises with accommodation – it was booked and there was no expectation about whether it was a conventional hotel, hostel, apartment, commune, or a tent. The walk from the station was unpopulated. Maybe because it was Sunday? There were some groups of young, healthy-looking types who were no doubt there to throw themselves off mountains and ascend vertical cliff faces on bicycles.

It seemed I had booked a room in an apartment. A shared bathroom with no lock, but a rather lovely balcony that looked across the back courts of other apartment blocks. From the ambience of the streets, it was clear that there would no partying that night – food on the balcony would be eating out. The streets were damp from intermittent showers but the hunt for food began with a slow wander. Clocking the location of a pizza place around the corner, it was early enough to investigate further. And further. And further. And actually a bit further. This part of Innsbruck was almost deserted. I had passed the same group of three student types several times – enough to be on nodding terms. They looked as hungry as I felt.

From country to country, opening hours of supermarkets changed – a strange thing to need to know but absolutely crucial at moments like this. There would be no abnormally potato-based salads tonight.

Forty minutes later, clocking that pizza joint location proved to be smart – the students had beaten me to it. The owner smiled as if to say *I saw you… I knew you'd be back.*

The skies were clear enough and the evening was warm enough to dine out on the balcony. A deafening clap of thunder sent some fellow balcony dwellers inside, noses pressed against the windows to see what would happen next. With a panoramic view of the Nordkette mountain, the rumble felt so profound that it seemed the following lightning flash would crack the craggy peak and tear the sky in two. And as the sky turned an inky blue, a tiny light shone out from the top of the mountain. That was the destination for tomorrow. A journey to 2256m above sea level, beginning in the centre of town. The underground station for the Nordkettenbahnen has a Bond-like blend of retro grooviness and Q-like technology. This first stretch of the ascent, called the Hungerburg funicular, was designed by architect Zaha Hadid and travels from the station across water and up the first stretch of the mountain, allowing passengers off at a series of stations.

To reach the summit takes another two cable cars, the kind that every time they go over over a pylon give a thump that could mean they have negotiated the workings successfully or they're about to crash into the mountainside. That's the thrill. When I was married and middle class we had several expensive skiing trips, where cable cars were packed with proper skiers and snowboarders and me pretending to care but craving a nice walk in the snow at ground level.

At the summit, the Haflekar, there are a number of small hikes but narrow paths, crumbling in places, coupled with amateur walking shoes meant they were out of reach. With sturdy poles it might have been possible – the kind that we all snigger at until they're needed. The solid path that meandered to the absolute summit was safe enough and meant that if my head wasn't in the clouds before, it certainly was now. Young women sat on the viewing platforms alongside high-powered telescopes, throwing their legs up to have coquettish pictures taken with this awe-inspiring backdrop. The chance to bring the tiny buildings of Innsbruck closer was unnecessary — getting this high means looking at the bigger picture. Being overwhelmed by this amount of sky doesn't happen very often. Before long we would all be back down to earth, with several bumps over the pylons and looking up at this summit. Without hiking, there's not much to do apart from soak in the rarefied atmosphere and have lunch. Never has a cheese toastie, salad, and apple juice tasted so good. With a few cocky crows swooping in for company, the black against the blue sky led to good photo opportunities, but they stayed far enough away to prevent a Hitckcockian scene of beating them off with someone else's walking pole.

These were moments that were a world away from life at home. True, in Dundee we have a fine hill, an extinct volcano that provides the city with its greatest natural landmark, but it doesn't need a funicular and two cable cars to reach the top, even though the view is also rather marvellous from its summit.

The trails were a little less challenging at the next cable car station down. Even if I took a tumble I wouldn't end up in the centre of town. I would only crash into the snow barriers that from below looked like matchsticks but up close were the hulking chunks of maroon metal. The trails were slim and one person wide, meaning an interesting dance when hikers came face to face. If they had proper walking shoes I would stand my ground knowing their grip on the slope would be less perilous. If they were dafties like me I would assess our relative fitness and occasionally give way.

When alone on the trail, I whistled. Actually whistled. There weren't any stretches flat enough to do a bit of a Maria and twirl, but it seemed as though the hills were alive, even if I had to provide the music. And I can't even whistle.

At the top of the funicular, the main station is sleek and futuristic but completely appropriate in that incredible landscape. It was based on the natural lines of a glacier and the combination of shape and construction material is perfect. Further down the mountain again it was time to hop off the funicular for a stop at the Alpine Zoo. The visit only lasted half an hour and was spent at the area devoted to the Fischotter. Otters have a large part of my heart, second only to Jack Russell Terriers. While I was happy to see that the wee fella was chomping away on a crab and had enough shade in this baking heat, I couldn't shake the fact that these were his confines. And while it was wonderful to see him so close, my mind strayed to a day on the

Isle of Mull where I might have required binoculars to see an otter feeding, but it was in the wild. Once he was done, there were no glass walls to restrict where he could swim. It was an expensive 30 minutes, but I had no appetite to gawk at animals in pens.

After nudging a couple of six-year-olds out of the way, gently, I managed to get to the front viewing window of the funicular for the ride down — a slow, smooth rollercoaster back into town. Disembarking with a disgustingly smug feeling that the early morning trip had avoided these colossal crowds, it was time to head into the old part of Innsbruck and see that yesterday's ghost town was something of an anomaly. There were packed cafés and restaurants, a shopping street with queues at every ice-cream stall, and fountains providing a welcome spray that vanished against baking skin.

Innsbruck had come alive. It was Monday afternoon and the mountain air had ramped up my energy levels, even in heat that required regular top-ups of water. One water stop offered the prospect of free cigarettes. Living in a country where cigarettes need to be hidden behind shutters and smokers are sent to the stratosphere to spark up, being approached by a handsome young man and offered a goodie bag containing fags, a lighter and a sticker saying I Love Smoking (something like that anyway) was a surprise. He also pointed out the range of ashtrays on display, not for the disposal of said ash but as a small museum to the joys of nicotine. Gracefully declining, it was necessary to explain my surprise at his generous offer and related how smoking is now treated at home. His horror was apparent and his dream of living in swinging London obviously dashed.

Having been saved from a rumbling stomach by the pizza joint the night before, it was tempting to go back. The balcony was calling, however, and the pull of a new supermarket proved too much. Even though it was another day of interacting with no-one but ticket inspectors and the cigarette pusher, I returned to the apartment with high spirits and a balcony picnic. Unlike the night before, the apartment had additional guests. Three teenagers who were sprinting from their room to the kitchen and back, giggling and generally having a marvellous time were in town to sit an exam the next day so this was as rowdy as they became. Being honest, they could have screamed and wailed all night after declaring that the trip I was on was *so cooooooooooooool*. Oh yeah. The kids thought it was cool. The night was still, the sun was going down on the Nordkette, I had some truly appalling Austrian wine, and all was well with my little corner of the world.

There was nothing to do but stare at those mountains, be distracted by movement on the other balconies, and eat enough cheese to mask the taste of the wine. The next day would take me to Vienna.

Innsbruck manages to be scenic from the train platform, with a ski jump clearly visible on the mountain. It was four hours to Vienna, with the ever-changing scenery far from shabby. Most of the journey was taken up with a strange one-sided conversation. An elderly Austrian man dressed in a proper Tyrolean hat, high-collared jacket and large Y-fronts pulled up past his trouser waistband would ask a question in half English-half German (but Austrian German, which is different – trust me on that), wait for my response and then laugh heartily, shake his head and sigh. Despite asking his name (in German) he never answered. It was heartwarming, passed the time, and endlessly entertaining. For him more than me it seemed. He left the train before Vienna (that's when I noticed the big pants), laughing, shaking his head, sighing, and adding the word Scotland into the mix.

It seemed impossible, but Vienna was hotter than Innsbruck. It was nudging 40 that afternoon, meaning the trudge from the Westbahnhof rather than the handier Hauptbahnhof was irritating, particularly as it ventured along one of those anonymous pedestrianised shopping streets. Where was the romance of Vienna? Where was the beauty? Where was the bloody hostel/hotel/wherever I was staying? It turned out to be a strange mix of hotel, hostel, and student dorm – but cheap for Vienna. In reception and in the room crucifixes were prominently displayed – it was best not to ask and enjoy the decent location.

With the temperature rising and no air conditioning, it was best to venture outside and experience the city that seemed to encourage nothing but superlatives. The streets around my accommodation were lined with creamy coloured buildings and it wasn't too far to the Nachsmarkt, a field of fruit and veg and other consumables. With no city map, wandering brought me into busy areas around the Vienna State Opera, which was festooned in giant pictures of Tom Cruise. The next night was the premiere of a *Mission Impossible* film and the opera house, more used to a soprano or two would be transformed into an IMAX Cinema for the night. It was difficult to see the building or anything of the square, as it was carpeted in crimson and blocked off at a distance with barriers. Barriers that hundreds of people were hanging over, watching workmen hang banners and make sure the carpet wouldn't trip up the star. Surely there had to be more interesting things to do in Vienna, unless they were claiming their place for the next day. I'm Scottish – I've seen people sleeping in London streets to wave at a woman in a sparkly hat going past in a golden coach – nothing would surprise me.

Whether it was the oppressive heat, the busy streets, or expectations that no city could meet, walking the streets was irritating and round every corner there was something else to infuriate me. Vienna was a prime example of a how a mood can dictate how we feel about a destination. It wasn't entirely my fault. Never have two cultural cash cows been milked in such a crass way. Turn one way and there was a life-sized (well you know what I mean) cut-out of Mozart offering a box of Mozart chocolates. Turn back and there was a wall of Klimt, with *The Kiss* on every conceivable houseware and consumable and wearable.

Around the cathedral the vintage carts, waiting to clip-clop tourists around the grandest streets, was a line of horses relieving themselves – pleasant odours in that heat. It wasn't the best. There was little to do but find a dark, cool bar and enjoy some local refreshment. Potatoes, cheese, and beer were immensely cheering. There were no Mozart mugs or Klimt cutlery and finally this was a small corner of the city I could enjoy.

The heat decided to stay through the night, prompting visits to the all-night shop nearby for cold water. In reception, guests were begging for fans or ice baths or anything to stop them feeling that they would spontaneously combust.

They were all at breakfast, so their fears were unfounded. The curse of the single person in a busy breakfast room struck again. Grabbing a tiny glass of fruit juice and laying it down with the plastic key card is usually a way to claim a seat before browsing the buffet. This done, it seemed safe to take time choosing a breakfast to suit the weather. So, carrying a plate laden with healthy food, I returned to my table to find my fruit juice and key pushed aside by a couple who were now in deep conversation. After a sleepless night it was difficult to walk away without saying anything, the problem being that English clearly wasn't their first language and my planned rant would have looked like a crazy woman ranting *blah blahdy blah* in broad Dundonian, which happens when I rage. Instead I sat at the next table (which was empty, that's right – empty) and sat far enough away from the table to make the gentleman have some difficulty when going on another pastry run to the buffet. That vengeance thing eh? That showed him eh? He had to send his wife...

Content that Vienna didn't live up to lofty expectations, I could relax and at least enjoy exploring this new destination. It's impressive more than lovable, grand rather than heartbreaking to leave. It was too hot for cake, and nothing really grabbed me as a memory or moment or place that would stay with me long after the journey. My mood from the previous day could only be lifted by a chum telling me to get a grip, so although I could understand why people would like the icing sugar decoration on the buildings and the shiny gold embellishments on the fountains, there was no soul to the city as far as I could see.

On the platform at Wien Hauptbahnhof the next day was the largest gathering of backpackers yet. The final destination for the train was Prague. The average age of the backpackers was somewhere between gap year and graduation. With a limited time away, they would be taking the most popular Interrailing routes. There wasn't a single occasion when taking out my pass in front of the whippersnappers didn't fill me with some pride. They would look at the pass, look at me, look at the teeny backpack and seem surprised – sometimes disgusted, sometimes impressed. By this stage, I really didn't care.

There's no doubt that there was a bit of jealousy on my part. With my background I hadn't even heard of Interrailing at their age. Gap years in my family would have been a euphemism for being on the dole. The fact that as soon as I was earning my own money I headed off to London for a week alone was enough to make me think that had things been different I would have had the spirit to do something like this.

Now the bulk of the backpackers were staring into screens rather than soaking in the life going on around them. My smartphone had been invaluable on the journey, for booking, train times and, ahem, directions, but nothing seemed to exist outside of the screens for them. Even in a group, the only interaction would be to show one another what was on their particular screen. At that point, even though I was the one travelling alone, I felt much more connected.

How can one take delight in the world
unless one flees to it for refuge?

Franz Kafka

THERE WAS NO real reason to leave the train at Brno. It might well be the
second city in the Czech Republic but before consulting the map in Vienna
to plan the next few days I didn't know it existed. I certainly couldn't pro-
nounce it (the simplest ones are the trickiest) and had not a clue what, if
anything, I would find there. However, heading straight to Prague after the
disappointment, bustle, and crowds of Vienna didn't feel like the right thing
to do.

Apart from a few people who looked like they knew where they were
heading, probably because they lived there, I was the only person who
jumped off the high step of the train. For some reason, as the journey progressed, the trains became more difficult to get on and off, to the point
where some guards were picking up old ladies who couldn't manage to get
a foot high enough to connect with the open tread steps. Not being particularly athletic, but certainly fitter than I was in Brussels, I backed off, half
turned, then took the leap to the platform. To the outside observer, it was
probably hysterical. Again, by this stage, I couldn't care less.

My hope was that Brno wouldn't be so huge that it would swallow me up
before I found the hostel accommodation for that night. It wasn't and the
hostel was one of those rare finds. It was spread over the two top floors of an
apartment building with a foyer that would find a place in any decent Eastern
European spy movie and, joy of joys, a lift.

With a price as cheap as the locally produced beer, the room was taste-
fully and simply furnished with a balcony window looking out on to the
cathedral square. It was part of a bigger apartment with a large dining kitch-
en and bathroom with a deep tub. Who knows who inhabited the other
room? Our paths didn't cross.

Brno was a refreshing tonic after Vienna. There was room to breathe.

117

There was space to walk and appreciate the buildings and the street art and the squares and the tiny, twisting alleyways. It was still baking hot, but not oppressive. It was unfamiliar and new and another one of those great gambles that sometimes pay off. At a market in the park, I summoned the courage to buy an apple. No common language required. I'll have that, here's some cash, thank you for the change. Smiles all round.

Arriving in each new country was starting to weigh my backpack down, in terms of loose change. By the Czech Republic I had reached the fifth currency, and had to find an ATM on arrival to withdraw what might be spent. It became clear that the amount withdrawn in Brno would last much longer than expected.

Chomping into a decent apple, the church across the square looked interesting enough to break the no-religion rule. Stepping inside the dimly light foyer, a lanky chap in a suit and tie ushered me inside and into a pew. I had crashed a funeral wearing multi-coloured trousers, trainers, a pink T-shirt and a cream sunhat – and with a half-eaten apple in my hand.

Of course it was too difficult to explain – speaking no Czech and with an ongoing service even a hushed conversation couldn't happen. The man was standing directly behind me and looking straight down the church. It seemed an ever greater insult to leave – more than managing to blunder my way in and intrude on a community's grief. In the end it was a pretty uplifting experience, even without understanding a word of what was going on. From the demeanour and age of the gathering it seemed like an elderly person had passed and there was a lot of laughter in front of the warmly lit altar. There wasn't much in the way of music, but when it did begin that was a cue to get out quickly, no matter what the minder thought. The last thing this family needed to find as they left was a strangely dressed stranger. I had taken the hat off, of course.

Standing across the street at a respectful distance, it was clear that a silver-coloured people carrier with curtains in the rear windows was the hearse, which the gathering followed. I had seen the car sitting outside before I went in but had just suspected a bit of cheeky parking. And I had left the apple in the church… I wasn't going back in.

Brno wasn't large enough to swallow me up but Špilberk Castle was a place where many entered and didn't leave. There was clearly something of interest on the hilltop and a slightly breathless climb revealed the castle, which had been better known as a prison. Prisons are fascinating to those of us who have never been locked inside one. In San Francisco countless visitors take the boat to Alcatraz. Visitors to the Tower of London are most interested in Traitor's Gate where prisoners arrived, the rooms in which they were held, and the locations where they met grisly ends.

The difference is that they are generally pretty busy, and even though the Alcatraz audio tour is pretty chilling, it's not as chilling as being alone in the freezing bowels of the prison at Špilberk while the sun rages outside. The dungeons are built with vaulted ceilings, the cell corridors are narrow, and it's difficult to avoid the bars that imprison waxwork figures in the cells – creepy in themselves.

Perhaps the most disquieting part is the section of the prison that was remodelled during the Nazi occupation of Czechoslovakia in order to create cells for their particular brand of torture, whether their perceived enemies stayed here or were simply in transit before being moved on to concentration camps.

The sound of footsteps behind made me freeze, but it was a young couple also satisfying their ghoulish fascination. Their presence was comforting and seemed to raise the temperature a few degrees. At the exit there was a fine display of souvenirs, including a Špilberk Castle yo-yo for a few Czech Koruna. Well, if you can't have some fun, eh?

Coming down from the hill it was easy to get lost in a network of alleyways and cobbled streets. It was also easy to be tempted by the pavement cafés and bars as it was clear that a decent meal wouldn't break the bank. Sitting outside a restaurant with a cold beer, I ordered a salmon dish that would have run into double figures at home. A quick calculation on a currency app showed that it was around £3. Obviously a cause for celebration, so why not have a glass of white with the fish?

As if the day couldn't get any better, two women arrived, one with a Jack Russell puppy by her side. This was clearly a sign to stay a while longer. There was another glass of wine, it might have been two – the glasses were tiny. Well, the dog was looking at me and paying me attention, even if no-one else was.

So, with a belly full of salmon, beer, and one too many wines, I handed over the equivalent of £10, which included a ludicrous tip. The night was warm, that deep sense of contentment that alcohol can bring had landed, and I was ready to try to communicate.

Earlier in the day, I had spotted a bar in a courtyard. Who knows how I managed to locate it. It was buzzing with groups of people enjoying large mugs of beer and standing around high tables. Beer in hand, all attempts to catch anyone's eye were either unnoticed or just ignored. Disappointing. However, leaving the beer largely untouched I had still time to explore further as the sun began to set.

Pretty squares that I had passed earlier were glorious in the evening sun and then the sound of live music drew me to an alleyway. Down the cobbled lane was a full stage and band, who then came off the stage and sang in perfect three-part harmony. Then I woke up.

It wasn't a dream. It was the last thing I remember that evening. The alcohol had a delayed reaction and hit me at the point where I had to get back to the room. I did but woke up with no recollection of how it happened.

At Brno station, bright and early for a long journey to Cesky Krumlov, I read a little about the city and cursed myself for missing the Brno Dragon. The legend of the Brno Dragon says that the people of the city were being terrorised by a creature they didn't recognise, but thought was a dragon. It was actually a crocodile that they managed to slay and its body is now preserved and hangs at the entrance of the Old Town Hall.

On the train and waiting for departure, I flicked through photographs of the city on my phone. I hadn't missed the dragon after all – there he was, snapped from every angle and remarkably well considering I couldn't even remember being there. Lesson learned. Watch the booze.

The planner had recommended that these journeys be booked. It wasn't compulsory but I didn't fancy standing. This was the first train with individual compartments and facing seats. And I had them all to myself. There had been no need to book after all – that was 90p I would never see again. Even at 8am, the heat was building. Every window was opened wide, the curtains were fluttering and there was little to do but settle and enjoy the five-and-a-half hour journey to a place that some people claimed was even more magical than Prague.

The line to Cesky Krumlov goes there and back – it has been created for people who really want to get there. The change at Ceske Budejovice showed just how many people did, including a group of young Scottish female backpackers and many Japanese couples, wincing at the slightly bawdy talk from the lassies.

The station at Cesky was one of my first experiences of clambering across tracks to get to the station, there being no platform as such. I had booked accommodation in the heart of Cesky. Again it wasn't quite clear what form it took, but this was ultra-cheap and smack bang in the middle. The walking route went straight through the suburbs. It was all downhill and at some points pretty steep, but that meant one thing. It would be all uphill on the way back.

When Cesky revealed itself, it was clear why people made the effort. Disney must have sent artists here to draw references for medieval Europe.

Rapunzel could throw her locks down from any of these towers and several handsome princes would come running. Entering through the town gates, the streets dip down again and take unexpected twists and turns. My room was above a souvenir shop and ice-cream stand. The stairs were the narrowest I had ever seen and the pack had to be taken off and carried above my head to negotiate the dog-leg turns. The room was tiny, it was hot, there was barely room for even my tiny backpack, but from the attic window was a view for which others would have paid a fortune – the tower of Cesky Krumlov Castle. It cost £19 for the night including breakfast. It was brilliant.

The castle was metres away, up a few steps that were lined with tiny galleries and shops that do well from the massive influx of tourists. It seemed like the most natural place to start. The castle is a massive complex of separate buildings, each bustling with escorted tours – not buses, Cesky isn't a day trip.

It lost its appeal at the entrance to the castle when, wondering why everyone was looking over the ramparts, I was horrified to see there was a bear in the pit. Not only that, but parents were allowing children to shout at it. It brought back memories of that school trip to Switzerland where, even in 1980, we were heartbroken to see bears in a pit in Bern. I had checked whether they were still there and, although they have been moved to Barenpark, an open green space on the banks of the river, it still doesn't feel right to have bears in captivity in a city. What followed was a half-hearted look around the exterior of the castle, but when I walked away my heart was full of sadness for that poor animal, stuck in a concrete pit for the amusement of people who don't give a damn about its welfare.

Thankfully there is more to Cesky. Each tiny alleyway reveals different ways to look at the town. There's an edgier side too, with an art centre that exhibits new work and also marks the fact that artist Egon Schiele lived in the town for several years. Wandering the galleries, I tried to find some sense in the more challenging works of art but preferred some of the graffiti art on the streets.

Following the Brno scare, there would be no booze in Cesky. I still had shivers realising there was a good couple of hours I couldn't remember. Sitting outside Zapa café with a salad and several refills of the sweetest lemonade I had ever tasted, this was a well-chosen vantage point for people watching. Well into the evening, the streets were busy with families, couples, and groups, generally from Japan or China and fulfilling the snap happy stereotype – not just with selfie sticks either. Each shot took a few minutes to set up and if it required holding up traffic by sitting in the middle of a street, then so be it.

Another thunderstorm hastened everyone's retiral to some form of shelter to watch the torrential rain in safety and comfort. Humidity through the night was oppressive but a fan purloined from the corridor was something of a relief and allowed a couple of hours' sleep. The heavy air and potential heat was on my mind when considering the steep climb back up to the station. Sleep had come late but hit me hard and waking was accompanied by a muddled *where am I?* It hadn't happened too often on the journey, but coming to in this strange attic room with the fan still whirring and a tiny letterbox-style window providing a strange medieval panorama, it could have easily been a dream. The trains were infrequent and, having seen how busy the incoming train was, it was a good idea to start the four-hour journey to Prague early. The accommodation had been booked and my contact there insisted on knowing exactly when I would arrive. Putting aside plans to stop off somewhere for a couple of hours and arrive in Prague later that day, I agreed to be there at a specific time.

The station at Cesky was deserted. The walk back up had not been anywhere as taxing as feared so, breakfasting from a vending machine, I had an hour to wait until the train. The sky was darkening again but the station made up for a lack of platform with a pleasant outside waiting area – and opened the bar for breakfast. I sat under the shelter with a juice of undetermined origin while a group of hikers arrived and headed to the bar. Another group of guys, Russian I think, sat close by, ate pungent sausage from plastic bags and produced even more pungent belches, followed by much laughter and congratulatory back-slapping.

The train was late. It was late enough that passengers hoping to get the next train had already arrived. There were no announcements, no signs to provide updates on when, or if, the train would arrive. Passengers stared down the track forlornly, hoping for a sign of life. Then the crowd began to get slightly anxious, bristling, with backpacks and suitcases in hand, ready to pounce when it arrived. When it did I had been at Cesky Krumlov station for the whole of Saturday morning. I used some valuable mobile data on the journey to tell the contact in Prague that I wouldn't arrive until around 4pm, which I did, pretty much on the button, despite the fact that rain was bouncing off the city streets as I arrived. My poncho was in the backpack and although I was wearing a fairly flimsy white T-shirt, it seemed wiser to hurtle through the downpour, knowing that I could change and have a hot shower while the rain passed.

The apartments weren't too difficult to find. Rain was running off the peak of my cap and my spectacles could have done with windscreen wipers, but I still managed to find the address. They seemed surprised to see me.

Despite the frantic e-mail exchange and the final *Great. See you at 4*, the receptionist looked puzzled and then worried. A man, who seemed to be her boyfriend, sat in the background, taking no interest in what was going on. She looked through her paperwork, glanced up, and said she was sorry but the room was not ready yet. It would be at least another hour. I was soaked to the skin, I had arrived when they asked me to arrive, and now I was being told that there was no room for me.

Her helpful suggestion was that I could leave my luggage and go out for an hour. When I pointed out that even though I couldn't possibly get any wetter, the experiment didn't appeal, she offered me a plastic chair. I rebuffed and huffed and went to sit on the cold concrete stairs; soaking and totally unchuffed. She approached me tentatively and offered a can of beer that I rebuffed, petulance rising by the minute.

I asked why there was such a delay and immediately wished I hadn't. This might have been exaggerated rather than lost in translation, but the response was that *The last guest did something bad in the bed.* I changed my mind about the beer.

From above there was the sound of banging, hammering, power tools, and finally a cleaner exited the lift with large bags of bedding. She was followed by a handyman carrying pieces of splintered wood. *The room is ready now*! The short lift journey was filled with trepidation. All seemed well, however. There were two pristine beds, a fluffy rug, decent lighting – all distracting me from the hole in the window, perfectly bullet-shaped. There was also a kitchen area. *This is your kitchen, you can cook. But the oven, she's not working, and the dishwasher is not good, and the cooker is a bit dangerous to light so it is better not to use.* Let's eat out then.

In the madness of the room and the crap kitchen and the bullet hole in the window, the weather had cleared leaving blue skies and an idyllic summer evening. Thank goodness. Being holed up in here with another potato-laden takeaway salad would have been more Ibsen than Kafka, not too suitable for Prague.

The book I had been reading when there weren't distractions like trains and bikes and trams and beer and other people, was *HHbH* by Laurent Binet, which told the story of his writing the story (if you get my drift) of Czech airmen Jozef Gabčík and Jan Kubiš, who were parachuted into the country during the Second World War to assassinate Heydrich, the Nazi man in Prague. They fatally wounded him. I was reaching the denouement where they, along with their compatriots, were trapped in the crypt of the Orthodox Church of St Cyril and Methodius. The church was surrounded by Nazis who were trying to flush them out of the crypt. The church was, by an absolute fluke, right next door to my apartment. On the side of the building, above the entrance to the crypt, is a brass memorial plaque alongside the bullet holes that took chunks from the stonework.

It was Saturday evening and, taking the route along the north bank of the Vltava, the streets became busier towards the Charles V Bridge, becoming unbearable when the pavements were so busy that a walk slowed to a shuffle past row after row of shit fridge magnets. Echoes of Vienna.

One overpriced Caesar salad later, a hawker of classical concerts at one of the churches grabbed my attention. Even though it was another tourist trap, at least it was an hour in the company of a string quartet and a soprano performing lovely tunes – that's my critical evaluation of classical music. It was soothing and value for money.

Encountering a stag party in the heart of the old town encouraged me to hit the back streets in an attempt to maintain my cello-induced bliss. The light was fading and, despite the fact that my apartment wasn't relaxing by any stretch of the imagination, I decided to go back, finish *HHbH* and, in the morning with the story fresh in my mind, visit the museum under the church and pay respects in the crypt where these unbelievably brave men met their end.

It took a few minutes to attract the attention of the man on reception at the church the next morning. He was lost in his newspaper and seemed shocked to see someone brandishing her entry money as soon as doors opened on a Sunday.

The story, told in Czech and English, followed what I already knew, but it was disrespectful and a tad crass to walk straight into the crypt. By the time I pushed open the heavy black door, designed to introduce the solemnity of what visitors are about to experience, the sacrifice that these men made was overwhelming. They knew this was a suicide mission but fought to the end, taking as many Nazis with them as possible. The only addition to the crypt is a series of bronze busts of the men who lost their lives and floral tributes brought by visitors. Leaving the crypt is difficult – not psychologically, it is really is difficult. The door has been designed that way to add to the claustrophobia and as a symbol of how trapped the men were.

After the dark and cold of the crypt, the sunny Sunday morning felt joyous. I had no guilt over feeling so upbeat following such a sombre experience. Respect had been paid but it was time to embrace the freedom and life for which these men sacrificed themselves.

The morning had passed quickly and, by the time I reached the Old Town

Square, hundreds of people had gathered to watch an old clock strike midday. It appeared that this was the famous Astronomical Clock – famous for doing interesting things. Things that held no interest for me, but watching the people waiting for the clock did. Settling down in a restaurant I ordered an Aperol Spritz, the first of the summer, and risotto. Yes, it was not yet midday but they didn't serve popcorn. The crowds swelled as the hands inched round to the position. Fancy cameras, phones, and even a few old school camcorders were held aloft in fear of missing the first strike.

I missed it. The drink had arrived but it came with a side order of wasp, chasing the sweet, sweet Aperol. When the risotto arrived, there was a two-pronged attack with the three-pronged fork, trying to keep it away from both. If anyone filmed this, it would have been amusing – a lone woman swatting and swearing under her breath. The wasp won and the white napkin was waved. As I stood up, lifting the plate and glass to find a table inside, a hand whooshed past my face and swiped that sucker right out of the air. The waitress proceeded to crush it, throw it to the ground, and finish it off under her heel. Talk about earning a decent tip.

A photographer was chatting up diners, motioning to them to cuddle in and have a snap taken with the Astronomical Clock in the background. The souvenir photo was ready to buy at the time they were paying the bill. It reminded me of those 1970s childhood holidays. At Pontin's in Blackpool the camp snapper roamed the streets, accompanied by someone dressed as a Muppet/cowboy/penguin/ghost, and took pictures of anyone who agreed. In the evening it would be a leggy blonde to sit on men's knees, but during the day it was generally something to attract children. A grown man approaching children with a cartoon character and taking photographs without a parent's consent. Then, hours later it would be in the shop. Families would scour the racks of prints and parents were bullied into buying the picture so it could sit in its souvenir folder at the bottom of a box for 10 years, only to be produced when the child's first partner came to visit.

She didn't approach me to be photographed with the clock. Obviously being alone meant that my experience wasn't as valid and didn't merit recording. I wouldn't have bought it anyway.

In the Old Town Square even the living statues had given up, their gold paint curdling in the searing heat as they sat on their plinths, chatting and having a cigarette. The heat was oppressive, making the crowds and the noise insufferable. It was time to escape to somewhere that would provide the romance and sophistication Prague had promised. The Kafka Museum south of the river was all that – and air-conditioned. It was dark but I'm sure it's how Franz would have decorated it. European museums can be inspirational when focusing on their cultural treasures, telling the human story as well as offering a journey into the masterpieces that the individual created. The gift shop had a decent range of souvenirs but they were tasteful and appropriate – no Kafka-shaped bottle openers or Metamorphosis mechanical bugs.

It seemed that, along with home-grown heroes, some Western figures struck a chord here in the days of restricted freedom. A wall close to the Kafka Museum and the Charles V Bridge has become known as the John Lennon Wall, daubed with portraits and lyrics as well as peace signs and other anti-war scribbles. It's a mess but obviously held some significance when the protest graffiti began in the 1980s. It no longer has that sense of rebellion – it's a giant scribbling pad now with teenagers writing their names and the date and breaking out the selfie sticks to take the kind of portrait that would have made Lennon spit. There are still a few peace signs and messages from the hippies, however, so hopefully the teenagers are taking those in.

Heading back across the river over the Charles V Bridge, Prague's great iconic structure was packed with ducklings following clipboards, Segway tours where people with perfectly functioning legs decide that it's preferable to scoot around town on the back of a vacuum cleaner, and stalls every few yards with caricaturists and keyring peddlers. Disappointing. Perhaps Prague is a destination for misty mornings, overcoats, and scarves – another time.

Let me recommend the best medicine in the world:
a long journey, at a mild season,
through a pleasant country, in easy stages.

James Madison – fourth President of the United States

POLAND IS MASSIVE. Huge. Heading too far into the country would add at least a week on to the journey. By now, with a clear head and having regained my sense of priority, moving to Abu Dhabi was off the table. There had always been a nagging doubt about the decision but over time I realised I would have been going for one reason – money. That wasn't enough.

This decision did mean that three months on the rails was the maximum I could afford, however, so for Poland it meant staying in the south of the country. Hasty research identified Wroclaw as a potential destination, but there were still two changes, making the journey roughly seven hours long. The compartments had facing seats that allow those travelling together to chat and enjoy the communal experience. With six individual travellers, however, there are six people trying to avoid one another's gaze. Unless you're a teenage boy who can settle back, stick your feet on the opposite seats and allow music to leak from earphones. The only thing to break the monotony were his whistling text alerts.

There was only one answer to this – Pugwash. I was surprised at how little music I had listened to on my journeys. At home I'm rarely without music but on this trip listening to language and being aware of what was going on around me was important.

The bass-heavy drone and the regular phone chirps were not a particularly rich chapter, however, so it was time for the Irish band to see me through the remainder of the Czech Republic and on into Poland. One song of theirs in particular, asking 'Where do I go from here?' and with the title *Answers on a Postcard* was particularly fitting. Writing postcards to the book pledgers gave me valuable moments to pause and think and make that connection with home.

An elderly couple joined us, the lady regarding me with good-natured interest. I smiled back and knew I couldn't begin to understand what they had experienced throughout their lifetime – a country being passed from one dictator to another then split into two separate lands. We can read reports, but these are people who have lived through it. And, as the foreign woman opposite got up to leave the train at Usti nad Orlici, the Czech woman struggled to get out of her seat, helped to untwist the woman's backpack straps and then, looking straight into her eyes, gave the younger woman a gentle pat on the cheek.

Whether it was the emotion of that moment – let's say it was that – I almost missed the connected to Klodzko Glowne. It appeared there were two parts to Platform 2 and being at the section where a train was waiting to depart made more sense than standing gawking at nothing in particular on an empty platform.

By this stage, even train seat upholstery was something to look forward to – it was deep scarlet on this sparsely populated train. It was clear there were no other foreigners. A father tried to control two boisterous boys and a single, older man had a wee stare at me when he thought I wasn't looking. There was nothing indecent, it was curiosity. When he left the train at a station that appeared to be in the middle of a field, he tipped his hat and waved a cheery goodbye.

At Klodzko Glowne, the last leg, there was no time before the Wroclaw train for even a quick look to see what lay beyond the station doors. In my compartment, there was a mother and son, probably five years old and restless. He grabbed my phone, which was lying on the next seat and ran away with it, straight down the corridor and away from his mother, who shrugged. With no idea what to do to retrieve the phone (I couldn't even search for *get a grip of your son* in Polish) it seemed my hulking presence walking towards him was enough to relax his grip.

Back in the compartment he took a small plastic saw from her bag and proceeded to try to saw the table at the window, the seats, his own leg, my arm... All I could do was look at his mother with wide eyes that said *Well?* Nothing, there was nothing. Until she exploded in a fit of rage and smacked him hard across the head. It was horrific.

On the last stretch to Wroclaw, I was alone in the compartment and wished I had booked two nights instead of one. Doing so little on trains was becoming more tiring than walking for several hours a day.

I had a hostel booked for that night. The street was far from promising but, like Brno, the interior was simple and stylish and the rate remarkably cheap. With only one evening and a morning to get a feel for the place, the backpack was abandoned quickly.

Reaching the Market Square, I was tempted to book another night – this was another fairytale location with quirky traditional architecture in vibrant colours that were even more appealing against the pewter sky. The square was dominated by a huge cinema screen and chairs. An open-air movie would have been a wonderful way to spend the evening but the cinema was deserted, with puddles being swept from each chair.

All through the main streets were banners and flags adorning lampposts declaring the city as a European Capital of Culture 2016. Before arriving, hearing that Wroclaw held that year's title would have prompted much head scratching. Being here, however, with my head swivelling at each new street and square, I made a mental note to return and celebrate with them.

At a restaurant on the square, with its candle in a wine bottle and a 50-page menu, I made a quick stab at something that wasn't red meat. Having forgotten to get a picnic for the trip, today's food had been a crushed wafer found in one of the backpack's side pockets and a bottle of water. Now for something hearty and Eastern European. The table was outside but under cover and, despite the rain, the light was angelic and the evening warm enough for a glass of white while waiting for whatever I had ordered. When it arrived, this still wasn't particularly clear. There was turkey, tinned peaches, some red rice of indeterminate flavour, and strands of pasta that might have been courgette. There was a sauce clearly destined for another dish, lettuce, and a single cherry tomato. Oh, and a pineapple ring.

Not even this culinary catastrophe could take the sheen off this place. It was a rainy Monday night and people were out enjoying the city. Getting slightly carried away, I lost my way a teeny bit and ended up in a slick shopping centre. A spot of sock shopping on a Monday night in Wroclaw was no longer a fantasy – it was actually happening. This was living the dream. A quick glance at the stationery shelves rewarded me with some quality Catholic tat for a friend at home too, with Pope John Paul II – Polish of course – featured on a range of notebooks.

It was dark when I emerged and, although the hostel itself was great, the street felt slightly less safe so heading back seemed a good idea. These grey stormy nights usually gave way to beautiful mornings, and so it was here. The buildings looked completely different against the cornflower blue skies, like the exaggerated colours on a 1970s holiday postcard. Even the Wroclaw Glowny station building itself, large and impressive and golden in colour looked completely different to the rain-soaked ochre hulk I had left the day before.

Trying to book the next leg to Katowice was not easily said or done. Quite reasonably I headed to the ticket window. There was a language barrier – I spoke no Polish, she spoke no English and she had not a clue what I wanted, even though I was giving great mime. The woman behind me was frustrated that some imaginary timeslot had come to an end, so grabbed my arm and pushed me aside. I did and said nothing, being taken aback that someone should manhandle me from a ticket window.

One strong coffee and mystery pastry later, it was time to try again. This time I approached an office where women sat behind desks. From the queue outside it was clear that we all had to wait outside the goldfish bowl until a customer left. Getting on the train with no reservation was looking pretty good right now.

Katowice was a smidgeon under three hours away. Katowice? you say. Katowice? I asked myself for the entire journey. But how could I spend a meagre one night in Poland? In the end it would be a measly two, but both entirely memorable.

The exit to Katowice station was through a shopping centre, but one with more soul than the Utrecht monster. I found myself on a busy shopping street and with another chance to meet my end via public transport. The accommodation choices had been sparse and I had chosen something with a pretty picture, a fountain with a building behind. Trying to find it, I became trapped in a network of underground passages that criss-crossed beneath a roundabout. To the outside observer I was a strange mole woman, popping up for a second, before realising I was at the wrong exit, and heading back underground. It was a concrete maze, a post-nuclear landscape with half-demolished hotels and a bizarre Soviet-style sculpture in the middle of something that, with less concrete and some grass, might have been described as a park.

This was 1970s Doctor Who territory. Any moment now, a battalion of Cybermen would emerge from another underground passage. Katowice is part of a region called Silesia. It even sounds like a planet Doctor Who would try to save.

At last, finding the correct exit, what appeared to be a giant flying saucer loomed large on the horizon. At any second a ramp would appear and the Daleks would motor down on to the concrete concourse. This was the Spodek, Katowice's gigantic conference centre. The name was a clue that I was close to the hotel, however, with the entrance tucked into a back street which could have been the deliveries entrance of a shopping centre. Inside the hotel the retro sci-fi vibe continued. I was Barbarella with a backpack.

The reception pod sat at the centre of a massive room, lit from above by circular skylights. There were seating areas with plastic chairs and sofas that were surely flammable, a gym, and the restaurant area – an interesting concept in open plan. Around the sides were the bedroom doors.

The room was brown. Again. There were strange string blinds at the window, and it soon became clear why. The flying saucer filled the view and a walkway for those who fancied circumnavigating the craft was right outside the window.

I had spent half an hour in Katowice, the fountain had nothing to do with the hotel, and yet this place was amazing – I needed something away from glorious town squares. It showed me that the feeling of euphoria a destination can provoke isn't necessarily attached to beauty. It's clear that Katowice is going through a period of change. There's demolition and reconstruction and, like so many cities around Europe, it is trying to find a way forward now that its heavy industry – coal, in this case – is disappearing.

The industry might be in decline but reminders of the industrial heritage are already popping up with the Silesian Museum and the area of Nikiszowiec, which used to be a mining community and has now been preserved as a historic monument.

The initial bleakness of Katowice softened into a city with pleasant streets featuring original street sculpture – a guitar player on a high wire sits high above shoppers. There are buildings, such as the Hotel Katowice that are clearly mid-twentieth century and deserve to be preserved as much as any Baroque or Art Nouveau exterior. There was an air of promise and optimism even if the city was far from being what it wanted to be.

Again, a lack of planning had thrown up a fascinating destination that wouldn't feature on any potential city break list, but the same lack of planning meant I could only scratch its surface.

With the interesting dinner from Wroclaw still sitting heavy on the stomach – it might have been bizarre but I did eat it – a drink was all I required. The evening was warm, the outside seating comfortable, and for an hour or two it was perfectly fine to be in Katowice.

The hotel was a different matter. The entrance by the bins still felt bizarre and the smiling receptionist in her central pod was sure to short circuit at any moment. Curious whether anyone used this central area, I grabbed my Kindle and took a seat on a sofa that looked more comfortable that it was – and it didn't look comfortable. I lasted about half an hour. In truth, it seemed *I* was the oddity, with other guests wondering why I was sitting on a sofa that could combust at any moment when I had a room to go to.

I left my Kindle in Katowice – it's not exactly leaving my heart in San Francisco – but I bet Tony Bennett didn't have several days of e-mail correspondence with his hotel to find out how much it would cost to ship his heart back.

Sing songs
every day.

Vince Keys

BRATISLAVA HAD ALWAYS been part of my rough itinerary. For too many years I had a plan to visit via budget airline, but now I was leaving the station and smiling at a massive Welcome to Slovakia banner. The station was basic and far from aesthetically pleasing but this large plastic banner was enough to know that the five-hour journey to get here was worthwhile.

An apartment had been booked and, according to the map app, it was 10 minutes' walk from the station. That didn't account for a strange tangle of flyovers that sent me up a set of stairs and along some abandoned tracks with rusting carriages. It was also in the opposite direction but at least past mistakes had taught me to tackle it early rather than wander aimlessly. Heading back and under the strange flyovers, the apartment really was 10 minutes' away. With no sign of the owner, I called the number on the e-mail and was told that his daughter would be there in five minutes. She was, in the company of a small Jack Russell Terrier, and if she thought I was an oddball I couldn't blame her at all.

While she was trying to show me which keys opened which doors I was on all fours, nuzzling the small dog and only half-joking that I would offer her more money if the dog came with the apartment for the night.

Booking a privately owned apartment meant an early check-in and a longer day in the city. Flying (or training) by the seat of my pants had led to some regrets but mostly it was paying off, with the most exhilarating experiences coming from general meandering and having no day-to-day itinerary. An hour into this latest urban safari, Bratislava already lived up to my expectations for no other reason than it gave me that all-encompassing sense of well-being. Then, walking through a charming courtyard, with galleries above, I could hear music. In the far corner someone was playing a piano.

As I drew closer, he paused after finishing a classical piece. Then there were the unmistakable chords that introduce *The Winner Takes It All* by

133

ABBA. The distance between my position and the piano provided just enough time to make the decision to do what my friend Ali encouraged me to do before leaving – sing songs. As the intro ended, there was the song's natural pause, and the young pianist must have been surprised to hear *I don't wanna talk…* the song's opening line.

He looked up, slightly bemused but seemingly delighted. As we carried on together we stumbled in places but managed to get back on track. It was intoxicating. I'm sure the vocal performance wasn't great, with rusty pipes and the high notes cracking, but I couldn't have been happier. It was totally freeing being able to sing without judgment, away from everyone I knew, and doing something that never fails to bring me complete happiness.

Those few minutes now provide an official happy place for dark days. The small square, the white buildings against a blue sky, the day being warm but not too warm, the fact that I walked into the square at the exact moment that the pianist decided to play one of my favourite songs – and one that I could make a decent stab at.

A crowd had gathered, but I was concentrating on this shared experience with a great musician. At the end he stood up and there was a quick hug – he spoke no English, I obviously spoke no Slovakian – but for a few moments we were connected by the shared language of music. Yes, it's corny but it's true. And the tooth? To tell the tooth truth, by this point no fixatives worked so it was snuggled in a safe place until seeing a dentist at home. I sang my heart out with that gaping hole.

Still buzzing from the impromptu gig, a wander brought me to the river, which I was surprised to discover was the Danube. A wide avenue of trees and fountains and cafés led down to the riverside, taking me past Hans Christian Andersen again, this statue commemorating his 1841 visit.

He's not alone. There are statues popping up from manholes, a paparazzi training his lens around a corner, a Napoleonic solder leaning over a bench. The statues are not particularly startling, but their positioning shows brilliance. The river is so close to shopping streets that there is no reason for anything to clutter the view, leaving the promenade free. I was a puppy who had rolled over and Bratislava was tickling my tummy. It was far too easy to fall in love with the city on a day like this. The architecture, apart from the quirky Blue Church, isn't particularly unusual or striking, but it's a city where anyone can feel comfortable. There was no fantasies about living here. I was already thinking about where I would live when I got back to Scotland, but it was fantastic to know that there were so many wonderful places on this planet to visit.

Following the duet, it was a day when being on nodding and smiling terms with other people was enough. There was no desire to instigate conversations – I was happily alone with no-one offering opinions on where to wander, where to eat and drink and no-one to raise an eyebrow when I wanted to spend too much time looking at what strange souvenir shops had to offer. There was a conversation in one of those, however. Buying postcards, the shop owner advised that I write them there, buy stamps, and post them immediately as he had petitioned to get a post box outside his shop. The whole story of how it happened was, well, it was long.

Climbing high above the old town to the castle was easier with a belly full of fish and a single white wine, the lessons from Brno having been learned. There were a few couples strolling around the grounds hand in hand, enjoying the romance of a dusky summer evening and the view across the river. Even when darkness settled, I had no thought of heading back. The streets were busy and even the cobbled back alleys felt safe. I wasn't ready for this perfect day to come to an end. Perfect is perhaps too strong. If the small dog was in the apartment on my return, that would have inched it to perfect. Either that or I had the winning ticket in the Slovakian lottery, with the TV draw show a fascinating watch before crawling to bed. The bedroom was up a small open-tread staircase and bijou to the point where I couldn't stand upright, so crawling is correct.

The next country had been decided, but to get there I had to head further east first. There would be one more night in Slovakia, with the most tempting city being Košice. It had been a European Capital of Culture in 2013 so there was a good chance that it wasn't a wasteland.

It was easier to negotiate the maze of flyovers on the walk back to the station, but buying supplies for the five-hour journey wasn't as straightforward. Rather than a shop there was a series of kiosks all selling the same products, apart from one that added hot pastries into the mix – with fillings unknown. This was a pointing exercise. Trying for water, she selected a two-litre bottle of something bright yellow, fizzy and packed with sugar. The effort was too much to try to change it so I paid for whatever this was and lugged it to the train – aware that the bottle was as heavy as the pack on my back.

The Slovakian train was smart and comfy and once we were off the guard came through each carriage with a free bottle of water (I know!) and a newspaper for every passenger. It was the day when the world had shown its disgust at the slaughter of Cecil the lion by an America dentist. Even though the words were a mystery to me it was clear the Slovakian press was equally appalled.

It was a shouty paper, a tabloid with headlines in capital letters where everything was a question or an exclamation! Messy design and pictures of girls pouting were far too familiar – even in countries that were new to me there were as many similarities as differences. I'm sure there must have been Slovakians looking at the paper as clueless as I was about some individuals who were deemed newsworthy for taking part in talent shows. It was a smooth and uneventful journey. There had been no missed trains yet – only a few delays and a couple of breakdowns, but no real crises. The countryside was pleasant rather than stimulating, but the memories of Bratislava were fresh and enough to sustain me until arriving in Košice.

With every passing day it became clearer that this journey would never have a steady rhythm so nothing could be regretted. If I made a mistake about where to go, where to stay, what to eat, how much to drink – they were part of the experience. It would be balanced out by the good decisions. Košice was a mix of both. The next day there were two choices of train – at 6am or 6pm. Only the early option would fit with a sketchy plan to get to Hungary.

Limited time certainly focuses the mind. The accommodation I had booked, which turned out to be the equivalent of a boutique hotel at home, was a short walk from the station, a walk that showed me I had made another good decision.

The receptionist was a well-rounded comedy character. Young, pretty, and with the fantastic broken English that lends itself to sitcom form, she was efficient, spoke incredibly loudly and, on hearing that my check out would be before breakfast, insisted that they put together a breakfast bag for me. I said it was fine, there was no need (the room cost so little) but I had paid for it so it would be happening. She then took a pen and paper listed the contents, reading them aloud.

Cheeeeeeeese. Bread. Yoooogooooort. Bread. Aipuuuuuul. Bread. Hem.

No ham please.

No hem?

No ham.

Why no hem?

Did she know a Ukrainian landlady in Rotterdam, I wanted to ask.

Satisfied with her list, she released me to the city. The main street or Hlavná ulica is a shopping street with no traffic, but it's no identikit pedestrian precinct. Traditional buildings house the shops, restaurants, and cafés. Looking down the lanes there are intriguing courtyards and shortcuts through to the parallel streets. Relaxed groups were cooling off in parks that cut through the centre of this main drag, with children squealing in anticipation as they waited for the water jets to start again.

Approaching the National Theatre, a fountain drew me in, siren-like. The Singing Fountain has dancing waters, but this is no cheesy Vegas display. This is understated, with gentle, melancholic classical music. It was now early evening and sitting on the steps of the theatre was enough to feel part of this communal experience. On the hour, a tree appeared to come to life and started playing music. I hadn't noticed that the tree was made of bells – a real-life fairytale. Slovakia was utterly charming and it wasn't over yet. There was nothing startling about these surroundings, but every layer of its history is there in the buildings, beautifully preserved and offering a hand of friendship in the attempt to know this city.

Working back from the main street was similar to examining the rings of a tree – the cobbled lanes with buildings that were probably worker homes are now galleries and small shops that never shout to attract attention but are more beguiling because of that. There are moments when its Communist past raises its head, with brutalist architecture. When they existed together as Czechoslovakia, these neighbours made up one of the world's most fascinating countries. I'm so glad I visited them back to back.

Choosing from restaurants along the main street brought me to an Italian for the first time. An exquisite meal for the cost of a medium takeaway coffee at home. Taking time over the pasta and one glass of red, I had a proper sense of relaxation and contentment.

Despite the early start, there was an evening to cover at least the main part of town. There are underground caverns that there was no time to see, but knowing they are there for next time is enough. Wandering twilit streets was bliss. It was the point in the journey that I realised the positive changes I felt wouldn't be temporary.

There was a temptation to take the 6pm train the next day instead but, looking at timings, any delays might mean arriving in Eger in the middle of the night. At 5am I was at reception. The station wasn't far and the route simple. What I hadn't realised was the breakfast bag might slow me down significantly. My receptionist friend had clearly added to the list, with the kitchen throwing in one of everything from the upcoming buffet. It was a breakfast carrier bag.

On the walk to the station I noticed a building that, for some strange reason, I had missed on the way in. Jakab's Palace is a couple of minutes from the station – a bizarre combination of Addams Family mansion and Disney castle. Deep emerald green tiles on the roof were glinting against a watery early morning sun and it was the final tick on my list that made a return visit to Slovakia essential.

It's not always easy to stand aside and be unable to
do anything except record the sufferings around one.

Robert Capa

EGER WAS ON the way to Budapest. There would be a couple of changes to reach it but, being at the end of a spur line, it had the promise of being a destination that deserved a level of investment.

There was a slight delay at Füzesabony, but it allowed me a quick clamber across the tracks for a look at the station. The further into this part of Europe I ventured, the more relaxed the safety rules became. Conventional platforms were rare with trains often arriving or leaving from the middle of a jumble of tracks. Picking my way through the sleepers and rails to reach a platform that was a few bricks wide was becoming the norm and pretty exciting. Small things, but each bringing a challenge.

The platforms were thinner, the trains were higher, the compartments were always a surprise, and the air conditioning came from windows pulled wide open with curtains flapping in the breeze if the train gathered any speed at all.

The trip from Füzesabony to Eger was short and there were a couple of fellow backpackers toting exactly the same pack. They were travelling for two weeks and I tried not to be too smug telling them that my pack was home for three months.

It was heavy at the moment. I had purchased some postcards and wanted reminders of Slovakia for my new place at home, wherever that might be. Cast-iron tealight holders from a blacksmith's gallery in Košice were a weighty choice but I could send them back, maybe even from Eger? Why not? Communication might not get much easier for a while.

The ticket inspector, once she been through the carriages, sat opposite and took a large bag of biscuits from her satchel. Before taking one for herself, she thrust the bag in my direction and smiled. Being touched at this communication I took one and she motioned that I had to take more. Surprised that it was my favourite flavour, I exclaimed *coconut!* which tickled her enormously and throughout the 20-minute ride she giggled, offered passing passengers a biscuit and screamed *coconut!*

At Eger I went to shake hands but was immediately drawn into a massive hug. She was around 4ft 10in and I'm around 5ft 7in, so it was an interesting embrace.

It was the end of the line. The train emptied quickly, as did the station. For once I had looked ahead a few days and knew I had to book a night train from Budapest into Romania. Fearing a repeat of the Copenhagen wait if I decided to get the reservation at Budapest, the empty Eger station seemed ideal. It was certainly entertaining. We got there eventually.

My fellow backpackers had spent most of this time staring at a station map, trying to work out where were we in relation to the centre of town. Sticking my head out of the front door it was easy to see why. The landscape had all the charm of an abandoned industrial estate and there was no connection to mobile data, so no maps. It seemed simple enough – straight on, turn right, and there would be a huge church before reaching the centre. It was straightforward, but much longer than I expected. Not the best day to be breaking in a new pair of walking sandals.

As with Cesky Krumlov, the route took me through the suburbs, with tidy houses and tree-lined streets that indicated a fairly affluent little town. Past the church, which turned out to be Eger Basilica, it was plain to see why a line had been constructed to reach the town. Not only is it incredibly charming, it's also the centre of Hungary's wine-growing area, famous for Egri Bikavér, better known to us as Bull's Blood.

The accommodation had cost £12 so I had no great expectations. It turned out to be a room in an apartment, which the lovely host told me belonged to her parents who lived directly underneath. The room could have doubled for any 1970s sitcom set. A riot of dusky peach and minty tones, I was ankle deep in forest green carpet but the minimal floor space meant the backpack was settled on top of a mini wardrobe for the night. There were three bedrooms, with families in the other two – we passed in the communal kitchen and dining area, silently. I even had my own bathroom.

The apartment was located on one of the lesser-visited streets, deserted apart from those keen on getting to the top of the Minaret. Passing the ornate basilica and an orthodox church, it was something of a surprise to see a 40m high minaret in the middle of a road. It's been here since the seventeenth century when the Turks occupied. This was the first location when the crossover between the Christian and Arab worlds became apparent. There was a bit of a queue to climb its 97 steps, where an iron balustrade protects those looking to admire the view, but looking up, nah – it was a bit low and flimsy for my liking.

The post office called, with a box and envelopes required to pack the bits and pieces before sending. There was a machine with numbers again, but this time the number depended on which service was required. Totally clueless, I grabbed one that had a graphic of a letter alongside it and was lucky. What followed was a lot of mime but the packages arrived safely.

The tourist office revealed the heart-breaking news that there were no bus tours that day of the wine area, called the Valley of the Beautiful Women, but it did leave me more time to explore the surprisingly grand town centre. They were so pleased to have a visitor that wasn't Hungarian, Slovak, German, or Turkish that it was a pleasure to speak with them. That is, until I was on the train out of Eger and they were cursed all ways that they hadn't told me about the newly opened Beatles museum at the Hotel Korona, mentioned by another passenger. I don't know what the connection is, but it looks great online.

While another Beatles experience was elsewhere, lunch was being served at a restaurant overlooking Dobó Square. Ordering what on paper looked like a light lunch of chicken breast, vegetable rice, and root coleslaw, this was a lesson in Hungarian portions. A massive plate of two giant crispy coated breasts sat alongside mounds of rice and slaw – and a teeny tiny 100ml glass of white wine – Hungarian of course. When in Eger eh? I settled in for the next couple of hours. This was too good to leave; give it time and I could conquer that stupid feeling full nonsense. It just needed another teeny tiny wine to accompany it. The final bill was around £6.

This was August 1, the first day of my final month and there was no doubt that my slow start in the north-west had eaten into the time. This wasn't an attempt to cover as many countries as possible, however, the journey was much more than putting pins in a map.

Sitting here it was valuable to reflect on how far I had come. Not just in mileage but in the decisions I had made. Today I had started to rent a flat in Dundee, found online, and viewed by my friend Shona. Even though I wouldn't be living in it for more than a month the tenancy had to begin today. It was something to put out of my mind for the moment, while having the comfort that I had somewhere to go back to.

Thankfully Eger was a distraction and even without hauling myself, two giant chicken breasts, a field full of rice, and an entire red cabbage up to the castle or into those churches, there was more than enough to occupy me and help walk off the gargantuan feast.

Along Kossuth Lajos Street are exquisite Art Nouveau exteriors – but the colours are richer here, less posh paint and more a box of fruit cremes from strawberry and orange to lime, lemon, and blackcurrant.

Food was the last thing on my mind, however. One thing that had changed was that I hadn't beaten myself up about eating such a massive meal. Generally the self-loathing would have settled in for the night by now, leading to a downward spiral that equated overeating to being a useless human being. But now I was just really full and hadn't dismissed the idea of a cooling ice-cream if the weather stayed the same.

Sitting in the square while the sound of an accordion drifted by from somewhere in the distance, it was apparent that this was the meeting place for couples, friends and families. A warm summer Friday night with ice-cream and laughs. Better than anything TV could offer. Later that night, the souvenirs safely with Magyar Post, some repacking was required. The room might have had ancient décor but the Wi-Fi was lightning fast. As night fell on Eger I cranked up the laptop, wrote some notes and listened to the World Service. Not everyone's idea of a rock'n'roll Friday night but again, better than anything TV could offer.

With pastries and coffee from a baker in the main street, a delay to the train leaving Eger the next morning didn't feel like hardship. The journey to Budapest was only two hours and it was a little frustrating that the train was sitting on the platform and, for a reason that no guard seemed to know, it would be sitting there for another hour. Fellow passengers had boarded already, but out here the air was clearer and the thought of sitting on a train with no air conditioning in the escalating heat didn't appeal. It was barely bearable even when the train reached some kind of speed.

It was a short ride back to the connection at Füzesabony, where a train delivered me into the melee of Budapest Keleti station around lunchtime. The apartment was booked for one night but the whole of the next day could be spent here with the night train to Sighisoara departing at 11.30pm. The shoes chosen for the past couple of days should have been absolutely fine for walking, but there was an unnerving friction and a slight chafing was turning into discomfort.

Having never been refused entry to a room on arrival – apart from Prague but let's not even think about that – it was strange to sit in the foyer of this apartment building. The receptionist busying herself with paperwork, I felt I was there for a job interview, woefully underdressed. It was ready, she was playing by the rules, at 3.01pm and I had access to what proved to be the swishest accommodation since Helsinki, but at a fraction of the price. Inspecting my feet before heading out, never a favourite pastime, there were a couple of small blisters causing the problem. Nothing drastic – uncomfortable, that's all. Still walkable.

The scale of Budapest was astonishing. Expansive, seemingly never-ending avenues with a grandeur that goes hand in hand with its historical significance. It has a transfixing quality that was a distraction from the increasing foot pain that was turning a confident stride into a tentative hobble. There was severe denial at play. As slick as the apartment was, how could I stay indoors when the skies were blue, the air was warm, and I was in Budapest. Budapest! The answer lay at St Stephen's Basilica. No, not the power of prayer, but the one thing I had avoided so far – sightseeing buses. There was no option. Carrying on would have crippled me, but a city tour aboard a bus followed by a visit to the pharmacy and some rest in the evening would prepare me for the long Sunday. Apart from an itinerary item on a press trip to New York, this was my first-ever sightseeing bus tour and as soon as the narration began it was clear how entertaining it would be – for all the wrong reasons.

A jaunty voice, located smack bang in the middle of the Atlantic, welcomed us on board and proceeded to trot out the usual facts and figures. When there was nothing to say, we had a few bars of *Nessum Dorma* or some eastern-flavoured pop music and then, as we passed The House of Terror, which pays tribute to the victims of the Nazi and Soviet occupations, the opening bars of *What a Wonderful World*. Far from being sniffy about the bus, it was ideal in terms of flagging up places for further exploration. It also allowed a cursory glance at those you're glad to have seen, but happier not to have wasted too much time on.

On board the bus there was a stern-faced youth who appeared far from in love with his job as driver. He had been slightly threatening when seeing my cold beverage in a plastic cup that might have come from a chain coffee shop and might have contained more sugar and cream than coffee, warning me NOT TO SPILL IT. Of course the idea was to hop on and off at different sites, but I had the hat and water so an open-topped bus, even in this heat, seemed like the sensible thing to do that day. Getting off might lead to getting lost and the inability to locate the next hop-on stop.

The nearest hop-off stop was still 20 minutes or so from the apartment but at least there was a kitchen where I could prepare an evening meal, a comfy sofa, and decent Wi-Fi where I could YouTube to pass the time while my feet were taking a break.

The apartment was definitely 21st century, but not too far away the supermarket had bright strip lighting that really did crackle and the shelves weren't overflowing with choice. There was a herb mister in the chiller cabinet but no access to it as an elderly woman was bent double giving everything a good sniff. It was clear that bent double was her natural state as she shuffled over to the watermelons and proceeded to give them a decent battering. Armed with a random assortment of edibles, I made it back to the apartment pain-free, congratulating my wisdom at taking the tour.

Sunday morning in Budapest had no pealing bells. The pavements showed some signs of over-indulgence from the night before, meaning a vigilant approach was required to Keleti, where I would store the backpack until tonight's journey. With a maze of roads, the underpass was clearly a better idea. At the bottom of the stairs were a few young men asleep on cardboard beds, a sight familiar in too many locations.

Turning the corner there was a campsite of hundreds of people. There were entire families who had claimed a small space, many with a tent and some with a camping stove. Others appeared to be eating from polystyrene takeaway boxes. Children were playing, men were chatting, and some women were holding tiny babies. I was aware that refugees were fleeing Syria but, having seen little news, my first indication of the scale of the problem was right here before me.

At that particular moment, the selfish question was what to do now? This was their home – the underpass to a railway station being preferable to the place they had fled – should I pick my way through the family groups and the tents? If I didn't, was I turning my back on them? Turning my face from the desperate situation that these people found themselves in. They looked happy. I suppose they were alive. Their children were playing and had all limbs intact.

The decision was to go on. Without rubbernecking, it wasn't too difficult to look around to see if there was anyone who looked as if they were in particular need of help. Heart pounding I emerged into the upper levels again, where a man spoke to me at the top of the stairs. He spoke some English and said that they were getting some help and supplies but there was a collection point for anyone who wanted to donate. My head was spinning at the prospect of carrying on with what now seemed a pretty frivolous journey. I was about to spend 600 Forint, about £1.40, to store a bag. What could that buy for them? All I could do was head to the nearest supermarket, buy as much as I could carry, and leave it to be distributed.

There was nothing to do apart from carry on with the day. Yesterday's

At the top of the world with regulars of the Nordkette in Innsbruck

Klimt with
your Klimt?
in Vienna

Puppy love in Brno

Evidence of seeing the dragon of Brno

The best view in town from a £19 room in Cesky Krumlov

You get what you pay
for in Prague

Gold melts at this
temperature in Prague

Colourful welcome to the culture of Wroclaw

The gig venue in Bratislava and the spaceship of Katowice

Magical evening in the side streets of Košice

Chocolate box architecture in Eger

Rare selfie on the night train from Sofia into Serbia

Money not blood at the bank in Sighișoara

Budapest Station toilet - I know...

World's longest curtains, commissioned by Ceaușescu in Bucharest

Picture of faith in Sofia

And the world's smallest funicular in Zagreb

Reading between the lines in Belgrade

The Baščaršija in Sarajevo
and (below) the delay at
Banja Luka

The unstoppable and unforgettable
Rusty Qui at The Hideaway

Beauty at every
turn in Florence
and Genoa (left)

Many kinds of blue in Nice

Not-so-fast
living in
Monaco

Tributes
to Oscar
Wilde in
Paris

Home in Dundee

bus trip had pointed to The House of Terror as a worthwhile, if bleak, destination. Grim it might be but long queues illustrated the interest. Like Riga's Museum of the Occupation of Latvia and the Documentation Centre and Nazi Party Rally Grounds in Nuremberg, these museums are crucial to remembering what happened in the not too distant past. These places are generally treated with respect, apart from the group of young Australians who couldn't wait to share some loathsome observations when walking through the reconstructed torture cells in the basement.

The squares of Budapest are filled with statues of heroes, generally on horseback brandishing swords to repel invaders from centuries earlier. For all I know the old woman who was bent double and battering watermelons could have seen and experienced things that make her as much of a hero for just surviving.

And still, while paying tribute to those in Europe who had been victims of horrific treatment, not 20 minutes away there were people looking to Europe to support them as they were forced to live in an underpass far from home to save their lives and those of their children.

There was nothing that could lift the mood of the day substantially. There were many hours to fill before the train that night, however. Whether my feet had genuinely improved or the distractions had masked the discomfort, I had no difficulty in covering the avenues around the Oktogon, the expansive junction with eight streets leading off. Note to self. Never drive in Budapest.

Having crossed the Danube over the Széchenyi Chain Bridge the previous day, a walk along the banks on the Buda side of the river ushered in the late afternoon. Back at St Stephen's Basilica, a pavement café was the best vantage point to watch crowds ascend and descend the white stairs. The night train to Sighisoara in Romania would take more than 12 hours and arrive in the birthplace of Vlad the Impaler around lunchtime the next day. A proper dinner was required and again Hungary did not disappoint in portion size. The combination of what seemed like a full turkey joint, eight potato croquettes, a tin of peaches, a single lettuce leaf, a slice of orange and a liberal dusting of cinnamon around the rim was no surprise now. Filling though. There were still a few hours to walk it off. It was around 6pm, the evening was glorious, and the streets felt safe.

Until, blasé with directions, I got lost. With no GPS. Not that lovely lost that leads into a side street where you find the best coffee ever. The lost that finds you limping in the pitch dark through an industrial estate, trying to hurry past groups of young men playing loud music, catcalling in Hungarian, and beckoning you into an industrial unit where they're doing, well, who knows what?

There were no taxis, but in the distance there was a garage. It was bright and welcoming. The attendant waved off any need for a taxi. Keleti was only 10 minutes that way, he pointed. It seemed right, there were railway tracks on the other side of the road but, on closer inspection, they were from an abandoned line. Why the hell did I listen? What I needed at the point was transport, not directions.

Standing at a busy intersection, I would have entered into a Faustian pact in exchange for a taxi – licensed or not. There was a tramline but who knew where that would take me? It was after 10pm, the train was leaving at 11.30pm, and I had absolutely no idea how to get to it. The decision was made to do nothing else until I had transport.

After 10 minutes there was a passer-by. She spoke perfect English and, shaking her head, said the information I had been given at the garage was completely wrong. I had to catch the tram across the street for four stops, get off, and get the Metro to Keleti. I didn't need to hug her. She saw the gratitude and fear and fatigue in my eyes and assured me I would get to Keleti with time to spare.

On the tram there were no ticket inspectors to deal with. It was three stops rather than four though. I had watched the line all the way and noticed a Metro station at three, where the bulk of passengers got off. Still, as instructed, I went to four, where there was nothing but darkness. The first nose tingle of a panic attack began to surface, but somehow I managed to breathe normally and hold it together. All I had to do was get back on the tram for one stop and keep breathing normally.

The Metro was bright and clean and beautiful and it took me to Keleti. I couldn't walk through the camp again. That would have brought the tears I had fought all day.

Make your feet
your friend.

J. M. Barrie

I HAD HALF an hour to spare. Finally I could admit that I had needed to visit the toilet for the past three hours. With the men's out of order, we were sharing. At this point it was empty, except for a male attendant who believed that the 130 Florint (30p or so) wasn't enough for a smile. I don't blame him. No-one would smile being there.

After trying every stall to find one with paper, I headed back to the cheery host who pointed in the direction of a single roll hanging at the entrance then watched carefully to check how many sheets I had the cheek to take. There was a sheen to the floor that I hoped sincerely was from a recent mopping. An armchair sat in the corner, held together by bacteria and sadness. As much as my feet were crying out for a seat, this would be certain death. The visit to the loo was a definite hover. Even after washing my hands, this was the moment to break open the emergency antiseptic hand gel.

There was a small but hardy group waiting for the train, with a few solo travellers including two young women. The carriage was more familiar to UK train users. I had a full table for four, which would prevent stretching out during the night but, being honest, I hadn't expected to have a full night's sleep anyway. Avoiding the sleeper option wasn't a financial decision, this was about the experience. My fellow female travellers were a German student who was visiting the significant Jewish sites of Europe for her studies, and a French woman who worked in a Parisian bookshop and was travelling for the hell of it. Both journeys were measured in weeks rather than months and they were surprised and slightly envious that I had the chance to take off for three months.

Not as surprised as a solo male traveller from New Zealand, who seemed shocked at any woman travelling alone, particularly in this fashion. He sat with two new friends who spoke no English and were fascinated by his digital camera. They had all had a beer or five and continued their late-night drinking session by visiting the buffet car that seemed to specialise in humungous bottles of cheap lager. As much as he obviously enjoyed the company of his new chums, he invited others to join, loudly and often.

I was lucky to be invisible at the next table seat and facing away, and the French woman took the brunt of the invitations, with her responses escalating from a polite no thank you to putting a coat over her head.

The overhead fluorescent lighting never dimmed but I wriggled into a sleeping bag liner, tucked my legs under the table and balanced them on the seat diagonally opposite. I tried to remove my shoes but it was clear that something horrific was happening in there, judging by their reluctance to come off. That was something to deal with tomorrow – in less septic conditions. With the sleeping bag liner and a neck pillow there were snatches of rest. If I couldn't sleep after a day like that, sleep might never come again.

The ticket checks and subsequent passport examinations on both sides of the border weren't particularly conducive to anything more than naps anyway. I was still wearing the waist pack that had my passport, rail pass, phone, and wallet close to my body. It felt safe but was also good for easy access when a scary man with a cap pulled over his eyes was staring at you in the middle of the night.

The large cheap beers had taken their toll on New Zealand guy and he snored loudly. When poked with night sticks by passport control, he came to, but slowly. Once he realised what was required of him, he brought the massive backpack down from the overhead rack, slowly. He undid the straps and zips, slowly. It took a full 15 minutes or so for him to locate his passport, even with strident vocal encouragement from the man with the big stick. There wasn't an ounce of urgency about him. I had all his anxiety watching the scene. Once he found the passport and showed it, he proceeded to toss it back in to the bottom of the pack and stuff the rest of his belongings on top. Somehow he managed to fall asleep again between passport controls in Hungary and Romania – and the whole scene played out again.

His friends had long gone. One much earlier, being forcibly removed when he didn't have a ticket. It was a long night and, although I tried to start a book I had bought that day (the House of Terror was the only place I spotted English language books), even the tiniest bit of action in the carriage was enough to distract me.

Sleep must have come, however, as a flurry of activity and new voices woke me to a sunny morning. We had been joined by another dozen passengers, all displeased that they had been thrown out of their sleeper bunks around four hours before we were due to arrive in Sighisoara. At first it seemed they had bonded well back in the sleeper section, but as the chat continued it was clear that this was a tour group who were travelling together from London to Istanbul by train. By the riveting chat about Ofsted inspections, it was also clear that most were teachers. And judging by the amount of attention that New Zealand guy was getting, most of them were single. In the light of day, and despite his hangover, it was easy to see why. Tall, sporty, with a mop of dark curls and blue eyes, the teachers were bewitched. As it turned out he was living in England and was also a teacher! How marvellous! The eyelash-batting created a slight breeze; until he mentioned his wife. They showed no interest in engaging in conversation with anyone else – certainly none of us solo travelling gals, but then the tour guide arrived to explain what would be happening that day.

There were no decisions to be made. He would get taxis at the station, check them in at the hotel and then, while they took the allotted 20 minutes to freshen up, he would arrange transport to where they were having lunch… and so it went on until they were back at the station tomorrow to move on. There was no point in being judgmental. I had been in a similar position on an escorted tour in India. Group press trips were all like this, but those were free so they don't count. The teachers didn't have to rely on a flawed inner compass to find hotels that they had picked at random from a booking app, but I wouldn't have changed places with them. Even after the previous night's brush with hyperventilation on a Budapest tram.

Despite my mammoth meal the previous evening and several litres of water through the night, the morning brought my first visit to the train toilet, which made the station facility a clean freak's paradise. Let's leave that one there. I did. Sighisoara wasn't too far away.

Watches were put forward an hour for the Eastern European time zone – the tour guide was certainly handy in reminding us all about that.

Waving farewell to the people they had chatted to through the night, the teachers waited for their taxis. As far as they were concerned they saw a middle-aged woman hobbling off with their Kiwi dreamboat, so I laughed, tossed my hair, and gave him a playful punch on the arm. He was frightened and got into a taxi. For some bizarre reason my decision was to walk the 10 minute journey to the hotel. Clearly the tour guide didn't think his charges should walk two minutes to the taxi rank.

The hotel room reminded me of my Gran Wilson's last house. There was a teak dressing table and a textured orange shiny throw over the bed with some serious flounces. It was quite comforting. It was the moment when the shoes had to come off. Soaking them seemed to be the best idea to lessen the damage. So, sitting on the loo with my feet above my head in a full sink, it struck me that it was far from the glamour that travelling through Europe as a mysterious lone female had once conjured up. When the shoes were loose enough to take off, it looked like game over. I hadn't admitted it to myself at the time but that final walk from the station was a test to see how my feet were. They were bloody awful. No need for graphic descriptions but there was a plane ticket home with my name on it. From where though? Bucharest was to be the next major city, six and a half hours away by train.

This was a moment when I had to reach out to home, with a pleading Facebook status for any help to locate advice. It came within a couple of hours from podiatrist Mike Black, a friend of a friend, and soon I was hobbling along the main street of Sighisoara to find a basin and salt to soak the blisters. There were two pharmacies, side by side. Communication was a problem but finally I managed to convince them that I didn't want to buy a single blister plaster, I wanted the entire box. The walking shoes from Bruges had split and been abandoned a few days before. With advice to wear shoes rather than sandals, I hobbled around town looking for a decent pair of shoes. Every pair of trainers looked like a fire hazard and I ended up with a pretty sturdy pair of grey ankle boots. They looked incongruous with lightweight trousers and a T-shirt but, along with the entire stock of Sighisoara podiatry supplies, they would get me to Bucharest. There would be no hunt for Vlad here and the next planned stop of Brasov would need to be skipped in case I did have to fly home. Every step felt like more damage was being done so there was nothing for it but to grab some supplies, retire to gran's bedroom, and find something on telly – a triple bill of *Murder, She Wrote* as it turned out.

The next morning, the 10-minute walk to the station had to be attempted. If that was too painful following a day of rest and pampered feet, a difficult decision might need to be made. They were slightly better, but as I arrived early to make the compulsory reservation for the train there was bad news. There were no reservations to be had and getting the next train meant being here for another five hours at least.

The train I had planned to take was due to arrive in Bucharest after 9pm – getting there five hours later than that was unthinkable, as was the prospect of having to sit there and wait. The time couldn't even be used to see more of Sighisoara – I was counting on another six hours of foot rest on the train. At first I sat in a daze, a gloom really, until an idea dawned. It was a remarkably clear thought considering my lack of sleep over the previous two nights. Between the heat and the real fear that I might have to abandon the journey, as well as electric shocks from the bedding, the previous night hadn't been peaceful.

I hobbled back over to the window and enquired whether the reservation was connected with my second class pass. It was. Did they have any first-class tickets left? They did. Well, I deserved a treat. It would get me on the next train and allow a little travelling in little style. The cost – a whopping £12.

Then the train was delayed by two hours. It would be 11pm at the earliest before arriving in Bucharest, so eating before the journey might be a good idea. The small station café was at the end of a corridor. Most of the tables had a single man drinking beer and regarding me with some disdain. I chose a soft drink and picked out a pizza from the display. The decision immediately felt wrong when the man behind the counter looked at the pizza and asked, *You want it hot?*

He brought a plate, cutlery, and napkin to the table and arranged a place setting – more promising. The pizza was given a full 10 seconds in the microwave before being slammed on the plate with plastic covering still intact and now melting. With a napkin in my hand to avoid injury, I peeled back the plastic cover with, it felt, all eyes on me. He had introduced the wrong pizza to the microwave, this one having a generous topping of something which resembled ham. The base was white and flabby, the topping questionable in every way, and the ambience hadn't improved. I put the drink in my bag and left the table. *No good?* he enquired. I had nothing…

Even the great sport of people watching had been exhausted when news arrived that the train was approaching. We could now cross the tracks to the platform and wait. The tour group was already there, standing in a circle. They appeared to be having a decent time, but I still couldn't understand why they had to stick together. Couldn't one peel off and sit on a bench for a while?

I knew first class wouldn't involve complimentary champagne and massages, but it appeared to be exactly like second class until I realised that, while second class had eight seats in a compartment, first class had six. That was the difference. Cool. I was on the train. Job done. Four out of six seats were occupied, my travelling companions being a young man and an older man and woman. Although most of the compartment doors were kept open to allow air to circulate from every available open window, the woman insisted on closing ours. It swung open and the whole frame was filled by a man who had been making a nuisance of himself at the station. It was our turn and there was no escape. Trying not to catch the eye is a skill and one that I clearly haven't mastered. A 'don't understand' shrug was no lie but it enraged him. It didn't help that he was extremely drunk. Then began a guessing game about which language I spoke, as he unbuttoned his sweat-soaked shirt to reveal a dapper string vest. He started with Russki then a few that I didn't understand. There must have been an involuntary flicker when he came to English but it seemed we were saved by the arrival of a ticket inspector. He didn't have one. Thank you, thank you, thank you... But rather than ejecting him with a stern finger wag, they had a cheery old chinwag and we were abandoned to Rab C Nesbit's bad-tempered Romanian cousin. His English was painfully adequate to ask me questions such as *Why do we drink alcohol?* He was more than qualified to address this, but at that point if any had been available I would have been happy to conduct some on-the-spot research. When he looked around and realised we weren't playing he hauled his bulk back into the doorframe and said *English...bah!* before spitting on the floor. His parting shot was to beat his chest and trumpet, *I AM NOT A MADMAN!*

This was the slowest train. Ever. The Transylvanian countryside was pretty, dotted with farmers working with horses and carts. The rhythm was soporific. Sleep could have come easily but even with no border there were several ticket checks in one journey. When it wasn't inspectors, it was entre-preneurial young men selling punnets of soft fruit and DIY air conditioning in the shape of bamboo fans. They would jump on at one station, try to cover as much of the train as possible and jump off at the next station before being chased down by the ticket inspector.

Once a journey is designed, equipped, and put in process,
a new factor enters and takes over.

John Steinbeck

BUCHAREST STATION WAS crowded with people coming, going, eating, drinking and just standing around, even after 11pm. The number of fast food places and a supermarket might have helped with this, but it was disconcerting following the lengthy journey with its heavy sedative effect.

This was the first night when a taxi was an absolute must. Between the late hour and the fact that putting my feet on the floor was again like pushing hot pokers into my soles and between my toes, I needed assistance to get to the hostel – after a quick visit to the supermarket. Healthy eating had gone out the window today and all that was required was wine and crisps. Large signs warned arriving passengers that unlicensed taxi drivers were operating at the station and to find the good guys we should follow this large arrow. It was pitch black outside apart from a welcoming row of yellow and black cabs. Before I knew it, the pack was in a boot and I was off to the hostel. There was no meter. *50 Lei* he said. Obviously those crafty unlicensed boys were painting their cabs in the same colours.

There was no fear for my safety. All this guy wanted from me was an inflated fare. And he wanted it quickly. With no seatbelt in the back, I rattled around as he took corners like a rally driver and joined in gleefully with the general chorus of beeping and shouting. The map had given a fairly direct route and to be honest I was delighted there was no pretence of taking a longer route to justify the fare. We made it. He made sure I got to the door of the hostel safely, I paid his 50 Lei and he screeched away.

It was a hostel with private rooms and, as late as it was, it was wine o' clock. It might have been close to midnight, but it was possible to sit outside among the other hostel dwellers, relax, and watch them stare into their mobile devices of various sizes and shapes. The revolution was clearly being digitised.

Whether it was the generous glass of red or the past couple of days catching up, I slept through the traffic noise outside, then through the alarm, and felt displaced and confused on waking. The grey boots had done their job up to a point, but I needed proper walking shoes if I was to survive the next few weeks. Did I really want to invest any further, however? Did I want to go outside at all? Would Bucharest get the short shrift that other destinations had when I hadn't been firing on all cylinders.

It made me wonder about every review I had ever read, knowing that the impression left by any destination had to be coloured by how someone was feeling on that day.

I couldn't walk far. I tried. I wanted to see the city and the best way, even though the bus had worked in Budapest, was on foot. Without properly supportive shoes, my chance of even making it back to the hostel was slim. I had done some research (first time for everything) on shoe shops and hailed a taxi to take me to the main shopping mall. This one was licensed, it had a meter and even though the journey was twice as long, it was a tenth of the price of last night's wild ride. The Unirea shopping centre is at a busy intersection. Although the architecture meant I could be anywhere in the world, there were hardly any shop names I recognised – always good. However, the new walking shoes were bought from a shop where I could recognise the brand. As much as I wanted the new, sometimes prior knowledge helped. These had to be good quality.

By this stage I was craving familiarity too. Trying to put all thoughts of cosy domesticity out of my mind in favour of living in the moment, I kept reminding myself that this was a journey that could never be repeated. If I did do something similar in the future, it would never have the excitement of the first time.

With new shoes on, deliberately chosen because they could be worn without any of that dastardly breaking-in nonsense, I crossed over to Unirii Square and wandered carefully down Bulevardul Unirii, which leads to Bucharest's most famous, or infamous, building, the Palace of the Parliament. Without wishing to show an interest in the Ceaucescus, the architects of so much misery, taking the guided tour seemed like a natural thing to do. It would give my limited knowledge some valuable context. The building itself is overwhelming in scale and even finding the visitors' entrance was baffling. The gate sentry pointed me to a door where tours were gathering. Being optimistic, I booked for the next day at 2pm, a full tour in English. I wasn't hobbling now but it was obvious my feet would need more rest that day if I was to achieve anything at all the next day. It was so bloody frustrating. I was fascinated by this place and wanted to make the most of the time. After stopping at a café for a salad, I hailed a taxi and settled in for the rest of the day at the hostel. At least there was an outdoor seating area where I could access Wi-Fi so this downtime could be filled with planning.

Whatever 'it' is, the past few days had taken it out of me. I was exhausted, not just by the heat of the day and heat of the night, but the pain and the effort, physical and mental, of getting from place to place.

There was no planning done. There was dozing, reading articles online, some more dozing and pouring the rest of the wine away, realising that it would only hinder a proper night's sleep. I had hoped that the morning would bring a better mood. Swigging from yet another bottle of water, I began to review the possible outcomes of going home now.

a) No-one would care if you went home now.

b) People would think you were a failure if you gave up before the end.

I had been away for more than two months, the length of time I had planned originally but then I decided to give up my traditional August gig of reviewing comedy at the Edinburgh Fringe for The Herald to extend the journey to three months, because it was more of a challenge.

You just can't hack it. Loser.

One thing about being alone is there's no-one to talk you out of making a bad decision. The downward spiral continued to the point where I had flights home on the screen and a payment card in my hand. My phone, charging on the side table, sprang to life.

I'll just book this, then get that message. Once the confirm button was pressed the circle spun and spun and spun and eventually the screen froze. Trying a restart I looked at the message.

How's it going sis?!

It was Linda, my surrogate wee sister, and someone who knows me well enough that I could be totally honest. I was...

Noooooo! Don't do it! Where are you just now?

When I answered Bucharest, she pleaded with me to meet up with her friend John, who lives there. I wasn't in any frame of mind to meet anyone, never mind anyone new, but she was already in the process of sending him my number and within minutes he was in touch and convinced me that we should meet. Once I checked that the flight booking hadn't gone through, I logged off, washed my face to refresh the red-ringed eyes, exercised my new podiatry skills, and prepared to go out.

The 2pm tour at the Palace of the Parliament was perfect timing for him finishing work at 4pm. We arranged to meet at the visitors' gate – I said he would recognise me by my green skirt and stupid hat.

The tour of the Palace of the Parliament was fascinating, of course. The building, architecturally, and in the intent of the Ceaucescus, is horrific. The largest public building in the world next to the Pentagon, Ceaucescu had one-fifth of central Budapest bulldozed to facilitate its construction, destroying most of its historic areas and displacing tens of thousands of people. The fact that it is so extreme in its ostentation, with marble and crystal chandeliers and specially woven rugs to fill ballrooms, makes it so chilling. It is still used as the parliament building. What else can they do? Waste the money that has already been spent? By opening the doors to visitors at least they can raise money and put the building in some context for tourists. Even on this two-hour tour we barely saw a twentieth of the building, which shows how obscene and bloated the egos were behind the planning.

The new shoes were working a mini-miracle and although the pain hadn't disappeared, it was certainly lessening. I sat outside the visitors' gate and heard a cheery *Lorraine!* John motioned to me to cross the road. Thankfully he had time on his hands. It was a wide, busy boulevard with no dedicated crossing so it was a case of taking my life in my hands and walking as quickly as my tootsies would take me.

You're right. That is a stupid hat. Beer?

I liked him immediately.

John recommended a bar I had passed earlier, one that had misting devices in the awning to help cool us off. I had recognised John's name from comments on Linda's Facebook page and she had spoken about him as a long-time friend, but the success of this too-brief encounter was the fact that we didn't talk about Linda at all. He lifted my mood powerfully and as I later learned, despite the fear of my state of mind dragging other people down, it seems that I did the same for him as he was feeling homesick for Scotland. We spoke about home but he was interested in where I'd been and where I was going and I was just as fascinated by what had brought him here to work for a charity. He ordered beer in fluent Romanian and made me laugh – I hadn't laughed for far too long. We spoke about the palace and he shared stories from colleagues who had been in Bucharest at the time the Ceausecus met their end. It was the perfect blend of silliness and intellectual conversation.

The chat had also made me determined to see more of the city in the final few hours I had there. I was so relieved that the flights hadn't gone through, I wouldn't have taken them now anyway. The evening was spent in the old town, where soft lights illuminated the restaurants and bars as the sun went down and somehow I managed to find my way back to the hostel on foot and without feeling any pain. The next day there would be a nine-and-a-half hour journey to Sofia in Bulgaria, plenty of time to give my feet another rest.

With a mini picnic for the day, I shared a compartment leaving the city with four young men from Huddersfield and a couple from the Netherlands. It was another baking hot day and as soon as a fan seller appeared at the door of the compartment he had my 5 Lei and I had a fan. The best purchase of the trip, apart from decent shoes of course.

Bucharest had been the first stop for the English guys. They had flown there a couple of days before and were hitting many of the capitals in the East, finishing off in Berlin in a couple of weeks. Although they were young enough to be my sons, I was delighted that they spoke to me like a fellow traveller as opposed to a mad old bat who should be at home watching *Strictly Come Dancing*. The Dutch couple also joined in with the banter as much as possible, making this the most sociable journey so far. Without Linda's interjection I might well have been on a flight home, feeling like a failure. Instead I was on a train to Bulgaria, sharing biscuits and laughs and looking forward to visiting Sofia.

Bulgaria had been my first foreign holiday, a school skiing holiday to Pamporovo when I was 12. We had flown from Gatwick to Plovdiv and head-ed into the Rhodope Mountains where I failed so badly at skiing that I was the only non-recipient of the Certificate of Competence at the end of the week. Subsequently I had flown into Sofia on a press trip, where a company wanted to show us a plot of land in Bansko where apartments would be built. Apart from that there was a lot of drinking and hearing stories about drinking, guns, and wild boar hunts from our host.

This time it would be different, whenever we got there. Crossing the border meant passport checks again, but we seemed to be stopped for an inordinately long time, with no passport checks happening. After an hour or so murmurings went through the train that we would be there for a while. The next compartment was louder than ours, with Americans and an older New Zealand woman, clearly a seasoned traveller who was sharing the scrapes that she had got into

I nearly had my bloody head cut off in Iran in 1973…

Travel one-upmanship was becoming an interesting spectator sport but she had served a Travel Top Trump right there, true or not. The message came through that we would most definitely there for a while. As we crossed the border we had to uncouple with the Romanian engine and recouple with a Bulgarian one, which hadn't arrived yet.

Gradually passengers left the train to sit around the platform and on the tracks. It was still in the low 30s but not as stifling as the low 30s in a stationary metal box. There was a water fountain, but more important there was a shop that sold ice-cream, water straight from the freezer, and large jugs of cheap beer. The Huddersfield crew went for ice-cream and water, perhaps recovering from the night before. The next compartment took full advantage of the cheap beer. Once we restarted the journey after a delay of four hours, it became clear they had bought supplies for the rest of the trip, which they had now named the Party Train.

We did our fair share of hanging out in the corridor and chatting but the beer smelled like turpentine and all offers of sharing were politely refused. There was a familiar face too, the German girl I had met on the night train from Budapest was also on her way to Sofia and being chatted up by an American dude – his description, not mine. There seemed to be no-one apart from backpackers on that train. A world of dangling straps and poor hygiene. Nearing Sofia, the party died down and travellers spread out to empty compartments to find spare seats where they could lie down and perhaps get some sleep. I surprised myself by doing the same. Lying in the semi-darkness, with curtains flapping around the open window and helping the warm wind to circulate, I knew that I wouldn't have done this a few weeks before. I would have felt vulnerable, I would have worried about what was living in the seats. I would have been sitting upright and judgmental. Now, using my neck pillow to keep my head off the seat (I wasn't daft) I drifted in and out of sleep for the last couple of hours.

The guard was making his way down the train, asking if anyone had two 10 Euro notes for a 20. It transpired that he had caught an Australian man smoking and said he would need to call the police. They had reached an arrangement. 10 Euros. The crafty puffer only had a 20. The guard was helpful enough to get him the change.

Travelling is almost like talking
with those of other centuries.

Rene Descartes

THE PARTY PEOPLE were already nursing hangovers when we reached Sofia in the early hours of Saturday morning.

The hotel, I could see from the map, was a five-minute walk away, practically across the street. With rested feet and it being so quiet in these early hours, I had no worries about walking there once we all found our way out of the station. It was a building site and getting to the exit took a good 15 minutes through underground passages and brightly lit concourses. I knew it would be dark outside, but this was pitch. Looking to the right there was nothing, just darkness, looking to the left it was similarly black, illuminated only by a red neon sign screaming SEX SHOP.

In front were taxis. Of course I paid over the odds again. As my taxi sped along the main thoroughfare from the station, the Huddersfield crew passed me in another cab, waving and giving me the thumbs-up. They had made what could have been a horrific journey a load of fun. Nearing Sofia I remembered that there was about £16 worth of Hungarian Forint in my bag that I would have to change. Knowing that Budapest was on their itinerary I offered it to them and after much protestation they accepted gratefully and said they would toast me with a beer when they got there.

Thank goodness it was a traditional hotel here. I would have hated to find a keycode or liaise with any individual owners at this time of night. The room was brown and maroon and cream and highly textured, but there were white cotton sheets and a telly to lull me into slumber. But at this time there appeared to be little except hardcore porn on normal telly. It was as enlightening as it was disturbing, and raised a few questions about how the human body works. Fearing nightmares it was time to switch off.

The few hours of train dozing paid off. Although I only had a few hours in

159

the cotton sheets, I was more than ready to tackle Sofia after a buffet break-fast that didn't differ significantly from previous destinations. The meat was perhaps more purple, but the cheese was white, the cucumber green, and the tomatoes red so all was well in my culinary world.

Driving through Sofia on the property press trip to Bansko, the host had been keen to stress how wealthy Bulgaria was becoming, with some random statistic about there being more Maybachs per head of population in Sofia than anywhere else in the world. At no point did he use the words Russian and mafia in the same sentence, however.

That was several years before and there was nothing to suggest that Sofia was turning into a European Dubai – if it was, the money was being well hidden.

It was time for another post office adventure, having been rebuffed at every attempt in Bucharest, part of Posta Romana training obviously being the quizzical look and withering stare. The post office just past the Lion's Bridge couldn't have been more welcoming. There was a bit of a party atmosphere in there. Between the manager with her small amount of Eng-lish, me and my cheery disposition, and the staff who were fascinated at the nonsense I was packing into a box to send back to Scotland, it passed an enjoyable half hour.

There was another night train to book, this time from Sofia to Nis in southern Serbia. The plan had been to stay in Sofia for two more nights, maybe using one day to get on a local train and explore somewhere a bit ran-dom, but the vagaries of the railway infrastructure mean that I was thwarted in that, having to get a train the next night at 8.30pm. I had already booked the hotel for the extra night so the money was spent, but at least it meant I had a place for luggage and somewhere to relax before the train that was scheduled to leave and due to get into Nis around midnight. Note the use of scheduled and due – there comes a time when train times become irrelevant and if there's any kind of flow – that's the one to go with.

Sofia isn't a city that can claim any one spectacular attraction – no Eiffel Tower or Coliseum – but there are ancient gems threaded through the fabric of the modern city.

The vastness of Eastern European destinations was hitting home and even though exploring on foot was the most interesting and had helped to shed excess weight, there was a danger that getting carried away along expansive boulevards could lead to the return of the hobble.

Despite single tickets on the Metro costing just 1 Lev, around 35p, it was a marked contrast to the railways. There are only two lines, but they cover a lot of the city. Shiny, modern, and sparkling but with a nod to the city's cultural history, riding the underground rails to navigate this city would be no hardship. On my way to the Metro station a flurry of white came in to my peripheral vision. A genuine Gypsy wedding with exploded meringue frocks and diamante glinting in the August sun. Moments like this and the other weddings I had stumbled across (and one funeral) were experiences that had never crossed my mind before the trip. Managing to share these everyday life events enriched the journey. Something to sit back and take in without taking photos – well, maybe at a discreet distance.

Taking the Metro for a few stops as far as Sofia University, this was an area that showed, a bit like Eger, how this part of Europe manages to bring together east and west without anything feeling out of place, because it isn't. Although the area is dominated by wide and busy roads, around the station there is the Banyi Bashi Mosque, built over natural thermal spas; the Sofia Synagogue, the largest in south-eastern Europe; the Catholic Cathedral of Saint Joseph, the Orthodox Cathedral of Sveta Nedelya, and the tiny Church is St Petka of the Saddlers, an 11th-century medieval orthodox church, now set below the road and part of the Metro station. It's separated by the dual carriageway from the watchful eye of Saint Sofia on top of her 22-metre-high plinth. She's only been there since 2000, taking the place of Lenin who used to watch over the city from on high. There was no great conversion here – I didn't go inside any of the churches but with so many faiths in a small area it showed harmonious co-existence.

Alongside St Petka is an enormous archaeological dig that includes another ancient church, the St George Rotunda. Churches and archaeology – both things I would flick over in any TV channel-hopping session – but the dig here was as sexy as the one in Turku, uncovering layers of a city that showed so much more than a flint tool. In Sofia they are revealing Serdica, a massive complex of Roman ruins with some parts so incredibly intact that there are plans to create an open-air museum.

Fearful of summoning an inner geek, it was time to head south on the Vitosha Bl, the main shopping street which, despite the presence of brutal buildings, has been softened by landscaping and on this day was busy with shops, cafés, and bars with awnings sending out those lovely cooling mists at regular intervals.

The school holiday in 1979 had been a revelation, with our blue jeans and rock'n'roll music and Coca-Cola all objects of desire. That's not a cliché. Locals really were trying to buy the jeans our teachers were wearing. One crate of small glass bottles of Coca-Cola had been sourced for the Western visitors, but knowing there was plenty at home my bottle was handed to a hotel worker. I'm still proud of that 12-year-old. Now, 35 years on, with the Iron Curtain being drawn back in the early 1990s, the rooftops around the square near the lumbering National Palace of Culture are dominated by neon signs for global consumables.

The evening was quiet and concerned itself with sleep. Having stopped earlier in the day for what turned out to be cheese and potatoes, there was no need for a meal. The next day would be another long one with the night train at 8.30pm. so there was no shame in cosying in for some strange snacks and channel hopping, trying to avoid the porn.

Waking up to glorious sunshine was becoming the norm and an early fill of cucumber, crusty bread, and highly unusual fruit spread was enough to send me out into the city again. With so many churches, it was strange so see anyone out on the streets on a Sunday but the antiques market near the Alexandr Nevsky Cathedral was busy and, in front, a newly married couple had stopped to have photographs taken with the ornate onion domes as a backdrop. In Slaveikov Square there was the magnificent sight of a bustling market selling nothing but books. Heading away from the book market I was a little bit lost, but just a little bit. This wasn't Budapest lost, a phrase now adopted to describe hopelessly, completely, and stupidly lost.

Lesson learned, there was no hesitation in taking the Metro from Vasil Levski Stadium to head south and back to the hotel, making sure I could pick up the backpack and head across to the railway station in plenty of time. Finding the platform was as difficult as finding the exit on arrival, but there was plenty of time to fill out the travel report part of the rail pass before boarding the train.

It wasn't there. It wasn't in the waist pack where it had lived for more than two months. This was what they meant by a cold sweat then. How the hell could this happen? One of the few things I had been so careful about. Holding back a few tears, there was only one thing to do, head back into the station in the hope that it had been dropped it in the shop when I was buying water. It was bulky though. The plastic cover now had three passes, the map, and a hefty sheaf of reservation tickets – it would have given a decent thunk when it hit the floor.

I was met by the sweet, sweet sight of the woman who had sold me the reservation the previous day. She ran towards me, clutching the pass in her hand. She was apologising for not handing it back after checking it was valid, but I was the one stupid enough to walk away without it – and then fail to notice that it wasn't there. I hugged her like I've never hugged before… True, I could have bought another pass for the final month but, despite the low cost of existing in Eastern Europe, I was still being careful now that the journey was running on the equity from the house sale.

It didn't matter that the train was, in good Scottish parlance, barkit. It was minging, filthy, somewhere a gourmand would have abandoned the rarest white truffle had it dropped to the floor. The journey was astonishing though. The sun was sinking over the countryside, giving the sky a pinky-orange glow. In the distance there were fires creating a blazing line along the hills; deliberate burning according to the only local person in the carriage. It was the land of dangling straps again and by this point my pack had joined them – it had been a while since I zipped the straps away neatly every time I got on a train.

There was room to stretch out but, knowing that I would be leaving the train long before it reached its final destination of Belgrade, I made an effort to stay awake until reaching the accommodation in Nis. The train had been delayed so that was going to be even later than expected. A few ticket inspections later, and with the Bulgarian passport control completed, I drifted off, not too concerned as there would be passport control on the Serbian side.

The reason I know that drifting off became a heavy slumber was the manner in which I woke up. Being prodded with the business end of a gun will bring anyone to their senses pretty quickly. At first I came to pretty lazily, however, peering at the big black thing prodding my upper arm. Standing over me was a guard and in his hand not the heavy stick I expected but a large black gun. Maybe it wasn't large, but to me it was massive. As soon as I sat bolt upright, clearly petrified, it went back into his holster.

He took my passport along with a bundle of others and headed off the train. It felt like an eternity until they returned and handed back each, freshly stamped. Then it was time to stand and watch as they took the carriage to pieces. Every seat was crowbarred apart, examined, and put back together. Floor panels were pulled up. A ladder was brought in. They took down ceiling panels and checked behind the live fluorescent strip lighting.

The carriage doors were next and then the connecting passageways. As they moved on to the next carriage, we were given the nod to take our seats again. That's one way to stay awake on a journey. It wouldn't be long until the train reached Nis. It was about 2am local time, but I had no qualms about taking a taxi from the station.

With the pack back on and surviving the leap from the train to the platform, there were signs to what I presumed was the exit. There was nothing there. No proper lighting, no cars, no buses. There was, however, a large gang of men who immediately began to catcall and walk towards me, making gestures that could be understood as hostile in any language. In my favour was the fact that trains tended to stay at a station for five, maybe 10 minutes. Sprinting back – it's amazing what fear can do for strength and speed – there was just enough time to clamber back on.

The guards were still moving through the train and looked at me with some bemusement, but no questions. OK, I was going to Belgrade now. The reservation didn't take me that far but rather the potential wrath of a Serbian ticket inspector than whatever was about to happen in Nis station.

I was woken again by the same guard, no gun this time but he nodded at my feet, which had found their way on to the opposite seat while I slept. He tutted loudly. Judging by the nick of the upholstery, my trainers would undoubtedly be coming off worse, but I didn't say that. The terrified mouse removed her feet from the seat immediately. He smiled. And winked. Winked? Mixed messages you cheeky bugger.

Not only was I without a reservation to Belgrade, I had nowhere to go on arrival, which would be around 8am. The only option was to head to the hotel I had already booked ahead to ask if they had something for that night and if I could store the luggage until check-in.

There was no more sleep that night.

In the aftermath of any war or genocide,
healing and reconciliation are ultimate aspirations.

Janine di Giovanni

THE HOTEL WAS directly across from the station. There was a room available that night and I could store the backpack with them. Before heading off to find breakfast, I had a quick visit to the ladies room, primarily to roll up my sleeve and examine any damage to my arm. Of course it was bruised. I bruise with the impact of a falling leaf or if the wind changes direction too quickly, so there was a peach of a bruise – a doughnut peach really, with the perfect circle of the barrel.

The events of the previous night had left me wired rather than tired, but the steep uphill walk to the centre of the city was a struggle. It was made easier by the cloudless blue sky and finding a pavement café that served freshly squeezed pink grapefruit juice and made a mean omelette. The coffee was black and tarry and exactly what I needed, even if it made me even more strung out. I hadn't been able to locate a map yet and, being honest, the getting lost thing was no longer entertaining. Now outside of the EU, the cost of mobile data was as eye-watering as the grapefruit juice. It was back to the old-school version of trying to work out where I was. This expansive shopping area had apparently been invaded by large robotic beings that I found out later were Transformers. I only knew that they made great photo subjects against Belgrade's pale Baroque architecture.

This was the first destination that had been part of the former Yugoslavia. While memories of the atrocities that happened in this part of the world fewer than 25 years ago were difficult to put aside, I was trying to focus on how the countries and the people were facing the future. On a sunny morning like this it was easy to do and enjoy Belgrade like so many of its citizens. They were certainly out on Kneza Mihaila, the main shopping street that is a mix of Communist-era grey and gems like the Hotel Moskva from an entirely separate Russian era. The pedestrianised area, brightened by colourful hanging baskets and an imaginative approach to paving, leads directly to the expanse of the Belgrade fortress and park, where souvenir stallholders laid out their goods, knowing that tourists would find their way here eventually.

There were the usual T-shirts and postcards and fridge magnets, but more than anything there were replica football strips, caps, and scarves for the city's two teams – Partizan and Red Star Belgrade. At the entrance to Belgrade Fortress, what must have once been a moat had been transformed into clay tennis courts. Was this commitment to tennis a reason for the success of Novak Djokovic, or was it inspired by the player, probably the world's most famous Serbian? His image is surprisingly absent from the city; there are no billboards with his sponsorship brands or references to him in souvenirs.

The city is divided by the Sava river, with its waterfront undergoing massive redevelopment. There are reminders of this across the city and, although it's ongoing, part of the promenade was worth a stroll to get some idea of the scale of the project.

Heading back to the area around the hotel took me past a park to the side of the railway station and in front of the bus station. It had become another makeshift refugee camp, but here families were out in the open. There appeared to be supplies of clean water and here they didn't appear as settled as the families at Keleti in Budapest. Many groups were carrying small bundles of possessions and heading towards the buses.

Heading up the hill behind the hotel, there were pleasant if not overly verdant parks where all ages were picnicking and kicking balls about. Higher on the hill was an unmistakable reminder of the NATO bombing raids – the shell of a government building, one of several throughout the city. Anyone would be disquieted at the extent of the destruction, particularly when a tram passes with a cheery *Slavimo Beograd!* logo promoting the waterfront development – the corporate future.

Being close to the hotel and fading fast now that the breakfast caffeine had worn off, it was time to check in and maybe have a nap before heading out to eat later. The good news was that I had been upgraded to a suite. The bad news was that it was the furthest room from the Wi-Fi router – getting a connection meant sitting out in the corridor.

Research and planning ahead were becoming more important because trains were less frequent and it appeared that my budget was going to stretch further. I was enjoying the showers that worked and cool white cotton sheets and air conditioning. That was the best. The heat seemed to be holding and, looking in the mirror, it was apparent that for the first time in my life I was looking not just fit but ever so slightly tanned, even with the sleepless nights and the stupid hat and Factor 50.

The early evening sun warmed the golden exterior of the railway station even further and a few lights were beginning to illuminate Savski Square. I set the alarm for an hour and settled down…waking just in time for a lengthy shower before breakfast. I wasn't chuffed but if my body needed that sleep, how could I argue? Once again I slept through an alarm, but then again I had once slept through a motorbike exploding outside my window.

Still slightly fuzzy from my Rip Van Winkle-esque snooze, I wondered if I was hearing things with loud tweets and chirps from the lobby. It seemed not. High above the lobby, built into an alcove, was a massive ornamental birdcage with several feathered friends of all sizes. It was horrific. How had I missed this yesterday? Surely not tiredness – I had managed to walk for at least four hours. Maybe, on top of the journey from Sofia, that four hours had resulted in a zombie-like state.

The breakfast room was an interesting mix of fellow backpackers who, like me, couldn't believe their luck at getting a room for this price, and businessmen, already uncomfortable in their suits in this heat.

Following an abundance of fruit and cheese, it was time to climb the hill again and find out what lay on the other side of the shopping area. Republic Square is regarded as the centre, where the national museums and theatres and statues of heroes are located. There had been some cursory research, however, and I was looking for Skadarlija, the bohemian quarter that's sometimes compared to Monmartre in Paris, as the place to find the city's artists and cultural shakers. Quiet streets and pavement cafés, dappled in sun through tree canopies, certainly seemed to be a gathering place for thinkers who fancied an early beer. I honestly thought it was later.

At the south end of Cetinjska is Pijaca Skadarlija, a permanent market selling food and household goods. It's not a tourist attraction, unless you fancy picking up some pan scourers and a massive bag of green beans. There's nothing quaint about it and, without previous experience of being stared at with disdain, I might have felt threatened by outright hostility. But those are the chances anyone takes when trying to get a taste of the real city.

Perhaps it was seeing people in extremis around the station the day before, but today I had no appetite to sit in a café and people watch. Belgrade had been fascinating and is clearly aiming to be one of Europe's prime city break destinations over the coming years. It's on its way.

Surprise is the greatest gift
which life can grant us.

Boris Pasternak

THE RESERVATION FROM Belgrade to Zagreb had been made the moment I arrived, in a queue of backpackers doing the same to their next destination. It was interesting to examine the other packs and spot the priorities. The young woman in front had not only hair straighteners in one of the external mesh pockets, but also curling tongs. My entire haircare package was shampoo, pony tail bands, the hat, and a comb. Then I remembered that these young people might be a little more concerned with their appearance, hoping for a few European hook-ups along the way. Even the thought was exhausting. Checking the departure boards was as fun here as it had been in Sofia. The Cyrillic alphabet is a thing of beauty, but shared numerals were the only way to check train times and platforms.

This Serbian train was rather swish. Clean, roomy seats in twos and fours with a central aisle and air conditioning. Unfortunately the seat reservation numbering was confounding everyone and, as terrible as I felt, I chucked an elderly woman out of what, for that journey at least, was my seat. Zagreb wasn't the final stop, this train was heading all the way to Ljubljana in Slovenia, as was the young woman sitting opposite. Marija from Skopje in Macedonia told me I had been wise not to visit her home city – yet. Wait a few years she said. She was bright and sparky and engaged with politics and culture. She was inquisitive and interested in the world and an absolute joy of a travelling companion. She also spoke to the woman sitting next to me, an elderly Croatian lady who was intent on feeding us as often as possible.

Marija was travelling to Ljubljana to see her boyfriend, a journey that by train would take her the best part of the day. But she had her work, which she could show me in the full knowledge that I couldn't read a word of Macedonian Cyrillic – whatever it said, it looked stunning on paper.

Behind me there were two young backpackers – a Finnish male and

Dutch female. They weren't together but they might well be soon, if the Dutch girl had her way. She was surprisingly vocal about the fact that she wouldn't be travelling if she didn't have her trust fund to fall back on. I was more concerned with Marija's life and her role in a student protest about the slum conditions they were being forced to live in. At the end of the journey I was genuinely sad to say goodbye to Marija, and on the day that she's sworn in as Macedonian leader I'll say that I knew her when.

Leaving Zagreb Glavni kolodvor, the hostel was on the wrong side of the tracks – the other side anyway. With no obvious walking route to get across, it was time for a taxi. The driver was delighted to hear my accent. I congratulated him on recognising it as most people had thought the lilt was Irish, but it seemed our kilt-swinging Tartan Army had laid good groundwork when Scotland played Croatia here.

The room at my hostel was a strange bunker-type affair located at the end of a lane. It was massive with a double bed and two single beds. It also had two washing machines, some interesting wall art, and a corner of mirrored tiles not seen since the glory days of 1980s discos. It also came with a free dog – a white fluffy wolf-like creature who wandered into the open doorway and settled down for a sleep. I couldn't shut the door but didn't have the heart to move the pup either.

Even though the taxi ride was relatively short, the hostel was a hefty walk from the centre. But there was a pavement bar outside – a place to have a drink and hopefully a chat. Marija had rekindled my desire to talk to other people. Unfortunately it was just me, Croatian lager, crisps, and the dog. Being honest though, I've had worse evenings.

My early morning walk located an underpass that led me back towards the station, which faces Kralja Tomislava. With handsome architecture on each side, the central park area also has impressive buildings such as the Art Pavilion, a building that appears to be covered in delicate lemon frosting rather than paint, and the Croatian National Theatre, which is more of a Cornish vanilla ice-cream yellow.

In between there is a succession of perfectly manicured parks with fountains, bandstands, and ponds. A signpost pointed out at least 20 tourist attractions, of which at least half appealed. I recalled the Dutch trustafarian saying she had already been to Zagreb and there was nothing to see.

If the Lower Town was a revelation, the upper promised even more. There was a tiny funicular delivering passengers to the spot where I stood panting and breathless – I might have been fitter but that climb to the Upper Town was tough and again it was searingly hot. I was rewarded with street after street of sights to rekindle the appetite of the most jaded traveller. In the spirit of only visiting more unusual museums or those that I felt some connection with, I had no hesitation in paying the entry fee to the Museum of Broken Relationships.

With a simple design behind the traditional frontage, each exhibit is an item donated by a member of the public and sits alongside a short explanation of how it related to a relationship that ended. It gave a sometimes heartwarming, and often heartbreaking, insight into the desire for lasting love. Some were hysterically funny with no-holds-barred vitriol towards the ex, others were distressing, showing a love that still burned fiercely despite the rejection of a partner. Anyone can apply to exhibit at the museum, sending their chosen item and tale of lost love. From a Snoopy plush toy and a dog's squeaky hamburger to clothing and baseballs, every story was brought to life by the presence of the item. To recover from the surprisingly emotional experience, the attached café promised that it sold *beers as cold as your ex's heart*.

It all seemed insignificant after viewing a photography exhibition at the Croatian History Museum. Most of the building was closed off for refurbishment, but this temporary exhibition called Faces of War marked the 20 years since Oluja or Operation Storm, the final battle in the Croatian War of Independence. It was the Faces, whether they were on the front lines or knowing that their loved ones were there and might not come back, that were truly heartbreaking.

One image called *Strah* or Fear, shot in Dubrovnik in 1991 by Pavo Urban, showed three men sheltering in an alleyway, perhaps from crossfire. One elderly man in a beret and holding a walking stick is upright and looks stalwart, another man is crouched with his head tucked into his chest and his hands protecting his ears from noise. The man in the foreground is seated on steps, pulling his dog towards him. It's unclear whether he is comforting the dog or the dog is bringing comfort to him. I suspect it was both. It's an image that has seared itself to my soul.

The entire Upper Town of Zagreb is a wondrous place, with the glorious exterior of St Mark's Church and its intricate tiling shimmering in the sun. Lunch could have been at any spot along Tkalciceva, but the views across the city from the area around the funicular station were even better. On the Strossmatre a stall provided a weighty vegetable wrap, with its neighbouring stall offering the welcome prospect of fruit cider.

Sitting alone at a low table it became clear that I was the subject of a conversation between friends in neighbouring seats. They were German but I was getting enough to understand.

When one of the men made reference to what I was carrying out front, not the waist pack but something higher up, I threw him a look that said I was on to them. They laughed and asked if I was German, I said no I was Scottish. Switching to English they asked me to join them, with the individual discussing my frontage patting the bench beside him in invitation. I politely declined and said I had plans. I did. To avoid him.

The four-minute funicular journey back to the Lower Town was more thrilling than it deserved to be. It led to the main street Ilica, a dividing line between the lower and upper towns and an awful lot longer than I expected it to be. When the directionless wandering starts, it's easy to get lost. Yes I did.

Perhaps it was down to distraction, already thinking about the journey to Sarajevo the following morning. There was one train a day. Miss that and it was go elsewhere or stay here another night. I loved Zagreb and it was in my mind to bring someone here. And laugh together at the Museum of Broken Relationships.

When you go to Sarajevo
what you experience... is life.

Mike Leigh

ONCE AGAIN MY arrival was much later than planned. The 9.18am train from Zagreb should have taken nine hours before depositing weary passengers into Sarajevo in time for dinner.

Back on a train with compartments, this one I shared with a Japanese mother and daughter, and a well-accessorised woman who I presumed was local, but as ever it's difficult to tell whether she was on an outward or return journey. Whatever, she was keen to communicate and pointed out highlights of the landscape at regular intervals. We crossed the border between Croatia and Bosnia at around 11.30am.

She became more excited, pointing and saying *Una, Una!* This was the river that acts as a border between the countries. This was one of the greenest areas I'd seen from the train window for many days. When we had crossed into Bosnia, I had tried to see the cover of her passport. No need. It was clear she was Bosnian, and proud. As soon as we crossed the border, she took off her saucer-like sunglasses and stared out of the window with love.

Along the river there were boys enjoying the sun and taking flying leaps into the water from makeshift diving boards. Away from the verdant park and stretches of water there was nothing much on the landscape of any great importance, to me anyway. The woman left the train at Novi Grad, not too far across the border. She shook my hand warmly before leaving and picking her way across the tracks in perilously high heels.

The train rumbled into the interior towards Banja Luka. The mother and daughter had put my train picnic of a filled sandwich and water to shame. A large case had revealed a feast of incredible complexity. With great ceremony, they proceeded to have an authentic Japanese lunch, to the point where I didn't want to catch sight of many things they were choosing to eat, being a tad squeamish about foods that once wriggled. However, it was worthy of applause – despite the difficulties of travelling, they were making the effort to eat healthily.

The train had stopped for a short while at Banja Luka, a modern station befitting its place as the second-largest city in Bosnia. Then it had stopped for a long while. Then it had stopped for an hour. By now, I knew the drill. There would be no announcement keeping us informed about the reason for the delay and when we would be moving again. And if there was, it wouldn't be in English.

Passengers began to get off the train and walk around the platform. Déjà vu? Following the delay at the Bulgarian border, I had no hesitation in trying to find out what was going on. It wasn't good. There had been a fire on the line ahead. The heat had buckled the rails and they needed to cool down before being removed, replaced, and then tested. I liked the tested bit. It could be another few hours.

The platform was now a sea of people, with one local man intent on entertaining us. His song could have been anything and in any language, with the slurred consonants and vowels favoured by every drunken singer around the globe. This performance was being fuelled by a cloudy liquid being swilled from a container that would usually contain car windscreen wash. There was a shop in the station foyer but, unlike the border station, there were no vats of cheap booze on sale. There was a fine range of junk food though and, even though the shopkeeper would have preferred Bosnian Marks, the station had no machine to get them, so Euros were better than nothing.

We wouldn't see Sarajevo much before midnight so I gathered up biscuits, crisps, replenished my liquid refreshment with something that was mainly sugar, and took it back to the compartment, hoping not to be judged too harshly by the clean-eating mother and daughter.

Delays were becoming a part of everyday life, so the only real frustration was the fact that it limited my time in Sarajevo, which was already too short. I only had one night, but arriving at the scheduled time would have given me just over 24 hours before leaving the next night.

There was time to stretch my legs and use the station bathroom to freshen up a little, before hearing the platform buzz that departure was imminent and by imminent they meant anything from a minute to an hour. Back on board, the Japanese daughter returned with an armful of sugar and chemicals that far outweighed mine. Some rituals are there to be broken.

We left Banja Luka after the usual routine where a man with a large sledgehammer would walk up and down the train banging a few rivets before nodding to the guard. The smell of the fire wafted in through the window, as did a soundtrack of AC/DC, drifting in from a park where bikers were having a bit of a picnic. We were so far south now that the evening sun was short and we were too quickly travelling in the dark. Houses were so close to the tracks that on this warm evening I could make out the faces of families on their balconies.

Despite the fact that we hadn't exchanged a single word during the 13 hours of being in the same space, as we pulled into Sarajevo the daughter asked if I was staying in the old town and, if so, did I want to share a cab? I didn't really – these things can get complicated. The decision was taken out of my hands at the taxi rank though. Licensed? Unlicensed? Who knew? The cabbies were in charge of this situation as they watched passengers emerging with dead-eyed stares of extreme delay and hair mangled from occasional dozing. I was halfway along the platform before realising I was still sporting a fully inflated neck pillow.

And so I ended up in a car that would drop off the mother and daughter first. It was the first night of the Sarajevo Film Festival and several roads were blocked off for red carpet events. The driver explained this and dropped the pair off a fair bit from their hotel, charging them 15 Euros for a 10-minute trip. Not great when you have their amount of luggage. He sped off again, turned right over a bridge, right again along the opposite bank of the river, took another right across another bridge, and right again, dropping me off about 200m further on from the previous customers. Then he asked for 15 Euros. This was scamming of the highest order and I wasn't in the mood to be ripped off – or regarded as stupid. If I had been in a dark alley and alone with the driver I would have paid up. But the streets were still busy, I wasn't far from the hotel and my backpack was in place. I took out 5 Euros and handed it over. Before he had a chance to argue I said, *That's enough. I'm not stupid.* I was still shaking a little at this out-of-character assertiveness as I checked in. The hotel was pretty sleek and echoed the bars I had noticed on the way. I hated to think it, but Sarajevo looked bland and another destination opening identikit bars for identikit beautiful people.

Following a solid sleep, breakfast was served on the sixth floor. Trying to maintain my fitness, I used the stairs from the first floor but had my way barred on sixth as the door, a fire exit, was blocked by oversized ornamental plants.

There was a reason this room was located at the top of the building and there were picture windows on every side. While I knew there had been a Winter Olympics there in 1984, and that winter sports needed hills and snow, the setting of Sarajevo was spectacular. The darkness had shrouded the fact that we were in a bowl surrounded by high mountains. In the morning light I was speechless.

The city still carries its battle scars – reminders of the Siege of Sarajevo, where Bosnian Serbs blockaded the city, allowing nothing to get in or out, including food and medical supplies. They also cut off Sarajevo's heating, electricity and water; photographs from the time show people gathering at the river for water and collecting wood. This lasted from May 1992 to February 1996. A tunnel was built in 1993 from the city to neutral territory on the far side of the airport, to get supplies in and people out but, despite this, more than 11,000 people lost their lives. The Kovaci War Cemetery stretches high up the hill in the Stari Grad area, one of the oldest parts of the city. It's inevitable that there is still sadness here but the people are campaigning to keep the human tributes. The Sarajevo roses, for example, are craters left by mortar shells that formed an almost floral pattern – they were filled with bright red resin.

Before the siege, it was best known as the location of the assassination of Archduke Franz Ferdinand, said to have been the catalyst for the outbreak of the First World War. The Archduke had just left the City Hall before the assassination took place at the corner beside the Latin Bridge. Nothing marks the spot.

The optimism of the city is shown through an exhibition in the reconstructed City Hall, one of the many buildings destroyed in the siege. This highlights the art, culture, and rich history that are as important as the anguish the world associates with this wonderful city. It did occur to me that the slaughter was only 20 years before. Where was my head at that time? I was a sub-editor on a daily newspaper for goodness sake. It seemed to be lost on too many of us. When I asked someone in a café how relations were today, he was reluctant to be drawn but said, *Well, the Serbs and Albanians – I think they still have problems.*

Despite all that, Sarajevo really is a joyous place, with the Miljacka river at its heart and the Baščaršija, an old bazaar that places Sarajevo at the crossroads between east and west. The bazaar has a fair amount of tat among the more interesting stalls, but its twisting network of tiny market streets are pretty intoxicating, even when the strongest thing that passes your lips is the oversweet mint tea. There was so much more to see but one more day would not cover it. I had to plan a much longer visit.

Being sober on a bus is, like, totally different
than being drunk on a bus.

Ozzy Osbourne

THE PAST COUPLE of weeks had been draining, physically and emotionally. It was time to relax for a few days. See some friends. Maybe pat a dog or two.

Of course that went against the plan to stay solo. That would have involved heading back north and visiting Ljubliana in Slovenia before, perhaps, travelling through northern Italy. There was a weariness creeping in, however, and the last thing I wanted was the final few weeks to feel like a chore.

I contacted friends in the Marche area of northern Italy and asked if they had any availability at The Hideaway, their escape near Amandola. They did, so the plan changed quickly to catching a ferry from Split in Croatia across to Ancona, then heading down the Adriatic coast. Getting to Split meant abandoning the train. It could be done, but it would mean retracing the nine-hour journey to Zagreb, staying overnight again, then taking a morning train to Split – arriving 28 hours later.

The bus was leaving at 4pm to arrive in Split at 10.30pm, but with the ferry leaving later the next day there would be a chance to leave my bag at a terminal and see a little of the first real seaside holiday destination on the trip. Even with the early start I had only had eight hours to see Sarajevo, not nearly enough, and taking a taxi to the bus station I tried to soak in as much as possible, but I had never been anywhere that I was so certain to return.

The metered taxi ride cost three Bosnian Marks, the equivalent of £1. Glad that I had shown a bit of spunk the night before, I gave this driver a 5 Mark coin and he was delighted to be told to keep the change.

Before the turnstile to enter the station, a man asked where I was going. Although I refused to tell him, he offered to drive me there for half the price of a bus ticket. Adventurous but not daft, I declined. It's not easy to escape from a moving car in the middle of nowhere. The single ticket cost £15. The concourse was as depressing as most bus stations, only with more people smoking. There were some backpackers around and, with an eye on the soft touches, a family sitting near the entrance sent their doe-eyed small girl off on her begging rounds.

Following a visit to the toilet (I'll spare you) which cost as much as the taxi ride, getting on the bus was a joy. Air-conditioned, not too crowded, and with some retro space-age upholstery that reminded me of a dress I had in the 1980s. Travelling by road does give a different perspective and, although I had been told that bus travel was probably quicker in this part of the world, my commitment to train travel was strong. Not 28 hours strong though. Once we cleared the outskirts of Sarajevo, the bus climbed and dipped through the mountains. Severe motion sickness was only abated by grabbing the seat in front and watching the road ahead through the windscreen.

The bus at least took an interesting route through remote Bosnian towns, collecting a few inebriated passengers along the way. One young woman in particular was enjoying her uninhibited state, shouting loudly and it would appear (I had no idea really) encouraging everyone to start singing. The woman in the seat in front of her turned and hissed. She actually hissed, like a massive cat. It worked.

And as we hurtled through the mountains, an earlier threat of a thunderstorm delivered torrential rain to windscreen wipers that were no more than adequate. It would be have been comforting to see them moving a little more quickly. Then it began to rain inside the bus. The ticket collector looked unconcerned. By the time he came to have a look it had stopped. Then it started again. He still didn't care. He hadn't been chuffed that I had held the bus up at the border, being a pesky foreigner who had to let her passport be taken away and stamped.

If accommodation hadn't been booked in Split, there were certainly plenty of options as people with signs offering Rooms for Rent met us from the coach. I had an apartment booked, one that I would be in for fewer than 12 hours – the bus was late. Calling the owner, we arranged to meet and I took a taxi from the rank. At first there was panic that I had no currency, then I remembered that I had already been in Croatia. Feeling confident after Sarajevo, I haggled a bit and the price came down to the equivalent of £2.80. He laughed and called me Braveheart. I said the Scottish football team would beat Croatia the next time they met. That made him laugh even more.

The owner came to the apartment. A woman with a particularly luxuriant head of hair for her age, with glasses perched on top and carrying a clipboard. From the off, I wouldn't want to cross her – there was a quiet menace that made me want her to hand over the keys and leave. She insisted on going through the map she provided, ringing every café and bar recommendation and stressing that I should say that she sent me.

The morning weather in Split was horrific and got worse. The key was soon back in the secure box outside the door with the apartment so memorable that the only photograph taken was of a shower curtain covered in cartoon piglets.

The ferry, which sailed at 8.15pm with check-in opening three hours before, was easy to find and close enough to make storing the pack for the day relatively easy. Not that I was particularly in a mood for exploration. There were roughly six hours to kill in a sodden Split, where holidaymakers wandered aimlessly wondering where the shiny ball in the sky had gone. The promenade would have been glorious in sunshine, but today it looked a bit sad. The streets of the Old Town had enough atmosphere that rain didn't dampen their charm, but with so many people attempting to negotiate narrow alleyways with open umbrellas, it wasn't particularly relaxing.

Food was the answer – an Italian restaurant with outside tables and awnings that could withstand the downpour. Around the arcades of Republic Square people sheltered to have lunch or just sheltered. Once in a while the rain became so torrential that everyone was cowering in doorways. There was no way the weather was clearing today and letting us dry off naturally. It's amazing how long you can spin out a plate of spaghetti and a rocket salad. In this case long enough to finish just before the awnings couldn't take the weight and collapsed, cascading water on to tables – empty ones thank goodness.

Even in the rain the raspberry-coloured buildings are pretty, but soaking feet and a poncho sitting in the backpack 20 minutes away don't make for the happiest of days.

In the less wet moments the crowds headed for Split's Roman ruins, particularly Diocletian's Palace. The ruins of the entire fortress make up the Old Town, so scholars of archaeology might be frustrated at how busy it can be, even on a day like this. The cafés, shops, and stallholders can only be delighted that they can operate from such a singular setting.

It was difficult to evaluate Split in these circumstances, but there was a definite charm that put a block on major grumpiness. That could wait for the ferry terminal. It seemed every passenger from every ferry leaving in the next 12 hours had given up and descended on the waiting areas. Checked in and ready for Italy, the only place to sit was a tiny bar with the world's most reluctant barmaid, or outside seating alongside cars waiting to drive on board. The ferry workers seemed surprised and slightly annoyed that they had to deal with foot passengers. There weren't many but us hardy few had absolutely no directions telling us where to board. We drifted together, thinking there would somehow be strength in numbers. We moved as one across the expanse of the port area and were directed up a small ramp at the side of the car deck. There were no cabins or sleeper seats available to book. It would be another night of haunting the upper decks. However, a new-found cheek led me straight into the airline seating area, where I stored the backpack. There appeared to be an awful lot of seats for the amount of passengers storing luggage – it was worth having a look for free seats later.

The morning couldn't come quickly enough. There would be a few days in the company of wonderful people. My friend Alison had taken me on a holiday to her house in the area a few years before and, thanks to Facebook, I had been able to keep in touch with the lovely souls that I met then. I hadn't met them all though.

There was Sarah and Mark, and Robert and Steve, and one little guy that I had heard so much about but hadn't met – a 17-year-old doggy dynamo called Rusty Qui. A terrier-type with three functioning legs, I had followed his exploits through his Facebook page and watched as Sarah and Mark helped him battle through so many bouts of ill-health. But he was still, along with their other dog Jessie, welcoming guests to The Hideaway and adding to his Friends list with every departing guest. I needed to meet him. Jessie too, but I'm a terrier girl and there was something in that little face and fighting spirit that was completely beguiling. I was so excited.

The ferry wasn't showband central but it wasn't Baltic Sea torpor either. Eating was becoming a way of passing the time now but the pizza here was darned good. A half bottle of Chianti later and the courage was summoned to head into that lounge and find somewhere to sleep. The place was awash with young men with man buns who looked like they did a lot of yoga. I inflated the neck pillow, looked out the sleeping bag liner and lay on the floor behind the chairs. On the floor. I could do a ferry carpet after Eastern European night trains. I could stretch out. And I slept.

I have found that when you are deeply troubled,
there are things you get from the silent devoted
companionship of a dog that you can get from no other source.

Doris Day

SARAH AND MARK were working in Pedaso on the day I arrived in Ancona. I would kill some time in the town until they were finished and then we would head to The Hideaway.

By the time the trickle of foot passengers disembarked and traipsed to Ancona station, it was just after 8am. Blue skies, a warm morning, and in a few hours I would be with excellent people and scratching dogs behind the ears. There had been a fair bit of small dog stalking over the previous 10 weeks. I missed my dogs. I missed them so much. I knew Dexter was happy and being well looked after by my ex, but at times I actually ached to cuddle him. Sitting on a sofa to relax meant having one cold side where he would normally cosy in. I had long given up apologising for my love of dogs – the deep affection for these four-legged creatures with small bodies but huge characters was as real as any other love. There was no way to know when a dog would be part of my life again, and in a way it would feel unfaithful to Dexter after saying goodbye to him the previous November. I had only cried for a month or so.

The train to Pedaso took around an hour. It was clean and quiet and efficient and really dull. This was transport, not a journey as I'd known it over the past few weeks. The town was still half-asleep, but hardened sun worshippers – they did have hides rather than skin – were already on the beach. Settling at the beachside café for breakfast, every time I turned there was another expanse of leathery flesh.

The beaches were furnished with tables and chairs and sun loungers. While the white skin of my watch mark made more of a contrast than ever before, there was no desire to join them. To pass a little time, I could lighten the backpack again and send some more tickets, programmes, leaflets and other bits and bobs back. The hope was that early morning at the post office in Pedaso wouldn't see too many other customers waiting in line behind me.

In the end it became a great entertainment. My teller appeared to be pretty clueless, no matter the nationality of the customer, and as I tried to communicate that the parcel was to go to *Regno Unito* and she looked back at me blankly, with the entire queue repeating **Regno Unito!** She was also a doppelganger for a previous boss, so a little bit of paparazzi stalking was required to send a photograph to former colleagues who despised the woman as I did.

Pedaso is a pretty town and deserved an extended wander, but come 1pm it was time to sit down, not for lunch after a late breakfast but for generous portion of gelato accompanied by a glass of Pinot Grigio. This felt like a holiday from the journey.

When Sarah's call came, I was relaxed and ready to catch up at the little slice of heaven that they had built up over the years. They had arrived here after running a successful pub in Yorkshire. They were looking for a challenge and found this one between Amandola and Communanza. Converting the tiny building for their own home, the former granary is now holiday apartments.

As the car drew up, Sarah came out of the passenger side. I put my arms out in greeting but she couldn't reciprocate – her arms were full of Rusty Qui. It was a group hug. Greetings over, we were soon heading to the hills with Sarah and Mark keen to hear details of the journey so far and me staring at Rusty sitting quietly in the footwell.

The first thing that struck me about The Hideaway was – absolutely nothing. No noise, no people, no distractions. The hills and the sky and a well-loved garden. There were no notes written in the next few days – this was the time to recharge for the final push. And, of course, relax to that point where the germs and bugs that have been held in abeyance for so long say, right boys, it's time to play.

Over the next day a flu cramped my limbs, left me with hardly any voice, and came with a complimentary blinding headache. I couldn't have had better friends while I felt so dreadful. The farmacia in Communanza helped with a combination of unfamiliar potions and, despite the amount of work they had to do with guests, Sarah and Mark somehow managed to look after me while summoning up the energy to attend a succession of social invitations, with Sarah always managing to bake an elaborate cake if it was a birthday gathering.

Despite the potions the flu had taken hold and, although I managed to fulfil the invitations too, I felt increasingly hellish. It was nothing that couldn't be remedied by sitting with Rusty, scratching behind his ears and his neck, then a quick belly rub when he lay down.

Rusty arrived in Sarah and Mark's life as a stray seven years before. He had appeared on the doorstep of Robert and Steve's home in Amandola in a sorry state. With all attempts to find his owner exhausted Sarah and Mark took him in, and with love and several hundred Euros, nursed him back to health.

Rusty also introduced them to Robert and Steve, who have become firm friends.

They found out that Rusty had been a ratter on a farm, sleeping under the house and living with the damaged leg since the previous owner neglected to have it set. Now at 17, he got around The Hideaway with his customary hopping motion and was a well-loved face around the pizzerias and butchers of the area. With two tumours, daily Valium for fits, and prostate medicine, his eyes were bright and showed how much he loved his little life. I knew I would adore him, but at any given moment my mind would wander to where Rusty was.

Three days of great food, laughs, and quality Rusty time passed quickly. From meals at the incredible La Conca agriturismo with Mirela, to prosecco and nibbles at the home of the lovely Monica (and a chance to meet her dog Nigel), to the always gracious dinner at Robert and Steve's home, where Rusty had a crap on the dining room floor. Thank goodness for floor tiles.

Unfortunately the flu hadn't passed. There was no way I could travel feeling like this and it was time to go home. Sarah and I looked for flights that would leave Ancona in a couple of days, hopefully enough time to get me over the worst and on an aeroplane without passing it on through the recycled air.

At the edge of the field, a young guest was throwing a ball for Jessie. Rusty appeared down at my side and proceeded to make his way on to the field giving a bit of a hoarse bark – I knew how he felt. In many ways I wouldn't mind this being my last stop. I watched that little dog throw himself around the field on three legs, knowing that only a couple of weeks before he had been so ill that it was touch and go whether Sarah and Mark would need to make that dreadful decision that comes to so many pet owners.

Look at him now.

Walking back to my room past the house, I popped my head in to say that I was carrying on, but would stay another couple of days to recover more fully. I couldn't tell them it was Rusty's doing – Sarah is as easy to tears as me and we would soon be blubbing.

The journey north would start on Saturday morning. On Friday evening, following another great dinner in Amandola, the crowd headed to the square to watch some entertainment. Still feeling slightly ropey, I sat in the car with the dogs, dispensing the pizza crusts and giving Rusty some serious ear scratches – making the most of my time with him. It had been an incredible week. Beautiful people and wonderful surroundings and the healing power of the four-legged friend. There were a few tears as I said goodbye to everyone, but particularly Rusty.

Robert and Steve were again so kind and offered to drive me to Pedaso and the first leg of my journey to Florence. Looking behind, Sarah was waving and Mark was holding Rusty high, helping him wave me off with his floppy leg.

> *Tears come from the heart*
> *and not from the brain.*
>
> Leonardo Da Vinci

THE FIRST MORNING in Florence began with the familiar ping of a Facebook message. I picked up the phone more quickly than usual, even though it was still the early hours. It was great to see a message from Sarah – just like her to check that I had arrived safely and that all was well.

It was Mark on Sarah's account. He had to break the news that Rusty had died the night before, a matter of hours after he waved me goodbye. Following an accident at the house of a friend, he had been paralysed from the waist down. Mark and Sarah could only make the right decision – to let him go. Just short of his 18th birthday, he had come to this untimely end and it was utterly heartbreaking. Reading the message once, twice, and a third time, I could imagine up to a point what they had been going through, but to lose him in this way after making sure that he entered his dotage as healthily and happily as possible – that's a kick in the teeth from the universe.

Although I couldn't have known, I had crushing guilt that, as they were making this horrific decision, I had been euphoric, falling head over heels for this city. The night before had been joyous. The final leg of the journey had been brightened by a chat with Leonardo, who lives just outside Florence and had some thought-provoking questions about the journey and the plan to write a book.

The hostel had been relatively easy to locate and, although the room was a bit hard and echoey and painfully red, it was cheap for Florence and only 10 minutes' walk from the main sites. The evening was just warm enough and even though eating on the Piazza della Signoria was more expensive than searching in the back streets, I wanted to sit on this square more than I wanted to save a few Euros. The lurgy was hanging around so an early night and a chance to recover more fully was required. Even though I still felt I was breathing through gauze and I wouldn't be singing any songs here, I was buoyed at making the decision to push through when it would have been easier to stop.

In Amandola it was the beginning of the Canestrale festival and, after burying Rusty in his favourite spot at The Hideaway, Sarah and Mark had headed up into the hills and watched the fireworks display. For Rusty. Why shouldn't they be? He was its oldest resident.

Mark's last message said that I had to try to enjoy Florence. And I did. As devastated as I was, what good would sitting in a hostel room all day do? There I would sit and cry. Out in the streets I would need to keep it together. If anywhere could provide distraction, it was Florence.

Another Sunday. The hostel had provided breakfast of a sort but I didn't have much of an appetite. A coffee and nearly new pastry was more than enough before heading out. This would be my only full day in the city and I intended to go back to the hostel when it was dark and I was exhausted. Spending five days in Marche had eaten into my time and I had already booked the Eurostar back from Paris on September 1. There was one week remaining to make my way from Florence to Paris. Spain and Portugal would have to wait until another time.

As much as a photograph can capture the undeniable beauty of Florence, no single image can capture the feel of this city. Even choked by thousands of tourists and with its share of tacky souvenirs, Florence somehow manages to retain its dignity. Breaking the city down into what you could say are its biggest hits, the Duomo Cathedral and Michelangelo's David, neither held any great fascination. The Ponte Vecchio had more charm. More than any other city, Florence seemed to be more than the sum of its substantial parts and becomes a destination that will take your heart and say, you can get that when you come back.

Heading over Ponte Vecchio, a triple Jack Russell spot certainly lifted my spirits I made the climb up to the Piazzale Michelangelo. The view across the city is almost too perfect. The same can't be said for the square behind. With a replica of David at its centre, tour buses bring those who can't manage the climb or can't be bothered. A few stalls repeating the same tat seem more intrusive being spread out over this square, rather than tightly packed in the streets below. Heading back down towards the centre, I stopped more often than I had walking up the stairs. Taking the more circuitous route back down towards the Arno river, the panorama of the city should be appreciated from as many angles as possible. Florence is a city that forces you to stop and look. Really look. It's the only way to realise that somewhere as beautiful really exists.

The food hall at Mercato Centrale provided my only meal of the day. There are no familiar chains – no stainless steel vats of flabby noodles or pathetic lettuce. The pizza looked extraordinary, but with no Rusty under the table waiting for some crust, it didn't feel appropriate that night.

Looking for distractions until bedtime that didn't involve alcohol or too much gelato, The Medici Dynasty Show and the Da Vinci Alive Experience were interesting options.

The Medici Dynasty show is a two-hander theatre piece that happens five times a week in the San Giovannino dei Padri Scolopi Library. The characters are the last two surviving members of the family, the Grand Duke Gian Gastone and his sister Anna Maria Luisa who provide a rundown of just how important the Medicis were, particularly to Renaissance Florence. The multimedia projections and surround sound that accompany the show are impressive, but at times I chewed my fist to stifle giggles as they chewed the scenery. Billed as the only English language show in Florence, it's the perfect tourist infotainment as the flyers call it. The restless teenagers, dragged in by their parents, might disagree.

The Santo Stefano al Ponte church was the setting for Da Vinci Alive Experience, which immersed the audience in images and music telling the story of the extraordinary individual. Whether it was the music, the sensation of which starts in the feet and travels through every nerve; whether it was the scale of the images that fill the peripheral vision; whether it was the realisation of the man's importance to humanity – it was exhilarating.

The Santo Stefano al Ponte is a short stroll from the Ponte Vecchio, even more beautiful against the jet black sky. It had been as enjoyable a day I could have hoped for. My heart was at The Hideaway, thinking about Sarah and Mark looking at the small corner of their home that had lost such a huge personality.

The walk back to the hostel at 11pm was warm and filled with a soft glow from shops that remained open to sell leather goods and gelato. No leather goods for me that night but the gelato was one way to end a bittersweet day.

Back at the hostel, the lounge area was busy. A film was blaring from the massive widescreen TV, but no-one was paying attention to Yogi Bear when they could be attending to their phones.

The next morning brought rain to rival that day in Split. The poncho was out, but dodging massive puddles on such narrow pavements was difficult and, by the time I reached the station, everything that hadn't been covered by the poncho was sodden.

The journey to Genoa felt so much longer than five and a half hours (with a delay at Pisa) as I exchanged a few messages with Sarah. I remembered too well the days after taking the decision to let a well-loved pooch go – the sense of loss is overwhelming. I still wanted to be there. They had supported and helped me through last week's illness and I wanted to do anything I could to help them in these dark days.

The decision to stop at Genoa had been half-hearted, as had the choice of accommodation. It showed as I arrived at a strange hotel at the top of an office building. The stairwells were stunning, however, and on each floor were officers of lawyers, doctors, and other professions that I couldn't translate. I had a room to dump a bag and escape. The plumbers had managed to get a shower room into a wedge, with the toilet at the thin end, taking up its whole width. It was straddle, sit sideways, or nothing.

My plan was to take a train to Nice at lunchtime the next day so, as uninspired as this stop felt, it was important to make the most of the time here. The rain had stopped but left a sheen to the roads, glistening in the coloured lights from the shop signs along Via XX Settembre. Crossing the Piazza De Ferrari there was no warning that I would be thrust into a 1950s film set. At any moment I expected Sophia Loren, with swishing skirts, cat's eye sunglasses and headscarf, to emerge from an alleyway. Perhaps it was partly the grey skies above, but there was something so wonderfully grimy about the streets heading down to the port. There was a romance to wandering these rain-sodden streets, even with a cough that was only slightly less hacking than a few days' before. Less lovely was trying to find somewhere to eat. Finally chancing upon a pizzeria, I headed in to dry off, even though it was more of a takeaway establishment with a few tables. As the sole diner, surrounded by sunny Mediterranean yellow walls and a fair bit of plastic fruit, it was surreal. Not exactly sun-soaked, just soaked.

The pizza was great (sorry Rusty) and startlingly cheap, with fresh ingredients under a carpet of lovely rucola. The pizza and a small wine cost as much as a measly side dish from any takeaway pizza place in the UK.

Boarding the train at Genoa to head into France was incredibly emotional. Italy had provided an absolute ocean of emotion. Until a couple of years before I hadn't visited at all – now I knew it would be a place I would return to for the rest of my life.

Anything happens in Grand Prix racing,
and it usually does.

Murray Walker

THE COTE D'AZUR arrived with blue seas and blue skies and a blue mood. This was the final chapter – my last country before heading back to the UK. There was no point in looking back and assessing yet. Being honest, it would be useless to ever consider whether it had gone to plan, because there was no concrete plan.

It was late afternoon in Nice and in the back streets, people padded by in flip-flops and swimwear, fresh from a day on the beach. That disoriented me. Too much bare skin for a normal street. Even though I was now slimmer than I had been in a few years and had even cast off the cardigan, I felt overdressed in shorts and T-shirt – and the hat.

The front desk gave a surly introduction, even though I tried to communicate in French. The room was a shabby box with a cupboard containing a wonky shower – a sleeping and washing cell, but no more.

The light on this coast is something rather special. It is gentle and soothing, particularly as the sun sets. Nice would be my base to explore a couple of destinations along the coast that were just 10 and 20 minutes away by train. That evening was just about Nice, however. Along the Promenade Des Anglais sunbathers were taking advantage of a seemingly endless summer evening, some swimming in the sea, some in an outdoor pool, others playing beach volleyball and the less active relaxing under blue and white beach umbrellas. Again I felt overdressed, but looking across the street made me feel underdressed. I should have been heading for a fabulous lunch with Elton, dressed in Chanel and walking a teeny tiny dog in oversized sunglasses – the dog, not me.

Getting over to those buildings was less relaxing, with three lanes of traffic in each direction, the palm trees on the central reservation softening the scene. The honey-coloured streets behind the promenade, with contrasting shutters and wrought-iron balconies, have more character than the seafront, which seems to be 20 shades of blue.

Again, the buildings are painted and even the cream-coloured facades look lickable. It might have been home weighing on my mind, but there was no emotional connection with Nice. Pretty, sunny, and in some places the architectural equivalent of shabby chic, it's a holiday destination and I didn't feel as if I was on holiday. There was no real desire to get to the heart of the place. While it wasn't a case of killing time before I headed home, it was enough to enjoy the colours and the warmth and the top-notch people watching. Along the Rue de la Préfecture there were bars and restaurants offering live music, which made a connection with the things I love, as did a massive halloumi burger.

The next morning, even though I skipped breakfast to get an early start, Nice Ville station and the trains appear to be permanently busy, allowing visitors to do exactly as I planned and take day trips along the coast. Twenty minutes away, Gare de Monaco wasn't the easiest place to leave but once the exit was located, I was high above the harbour. So high in fact, that looking down could be difficult for someone with vertigo. On yet another roasting day, maybe heading down towards the water would provide some fresher air. It was a steep decline felt most keenly in my thigh muscles. Of course, Monaco is technically another country, a principality at least, with its capital Monte Carlo built high on the rocks from the harbour. With no interest in the Grimaldi royal family, the palace, the cathedral, or the grave of Grace Kelly, there was only one reason to visit Monte Carlo – to walk the Formula 1 street track.

At almost 3.4km, it was a decent hike and being a street track had the added benefit of acting as a self-guided tour around the area. To walk the corners and stand on the start/finish line was exhilarating but this was one of the few places that I would have like to have shared the experience, this time with my ex-partner, who never misses a race. Even he would have been surprised at those (usually) men treating this as something of a pilgrimage and dressed in the expensive official gear of their favourite constructor and staring dreamily into the window of the Automobile Club de Monaco.

The tourist map of Monaco shows the track in grey. Thank goodness, as on the ground, without the red and white track markings giving clues, it's more difficult than I thought to know where to turn next. Even I couldn't get lost on a race track. Could I?

The old town area is again pretty, but pretty characterless. It's not a place that buzzes with pavement cafés. Of course there are people who live in these apartments without huge fortunes, but it feels like a place built to facilitate big Euros. Looking back across the harbour from the first climb of the race track, it looks dated. A place where older men in blazers would stroll arm-in-arm with much younger women toting several large bags, all advertising their designer contents. They would retire to the yacht later.

Maybe if I hadn't had so many weeks of experiences with real depth, it wouldn't have seemed so artificial, so constructed for a purpose. On my way back to Nice, there was Beaulieu Sur Mer, which looked like a film location and in fact had been. It was one of the backdrops for *Dirty Rotten Scoundrels*, a Steve Martin and Michael Caine film about shysters trying to con wealthy women. It was dozing rather than sleepy. At hotels looking out on admittedly startling waters, big hats and sunglasses were de rigueur. I stopped at a park with a pretty bandstand for a while and watched the population gather for afternoon chats. While I brought the average age down significantly, it did strike me that there were worse places to retire. There was even a Jack Russell Terrier under the table.

Back in Nice, I had warmed to the area a little. Wandering the streets at night helped. Like Florence, there was something about the glow of the signs from bars that created such a different atmosphere once the sun went down. At one point I spotted a small terrier trotting along the street. The little chap was alone and wore no collar, but was walking with a real sense of purpose. There was no way I could leave a collarless terrier wandering the streets alone so I followed. He crossed small streets, negotiated corners and finally, five minutes later, walked into a deli, where he was greeted with some enthusiasm but left empty-pawed. There might have been a quick treat involved, however. He turned back and retraced his steps, finally turning into a small gallery, where I popped my head in.

Votre chien?

Ah oui…

That's OK then. It seems even the dogs are fussy about the quality of their food.

One never reaches home, but wherever friendly paths intersect
the whole world looks like home for a time.

Hermann Hesse

PARIS HAD NEVER been part of even my most perfunctory plan. It had the starting point of Brussels and an end at the Gare du Lorraine, but as the journey went on that felt increasingly pretentious. Researching how to get to the station also showed that there's nothing there. The station is regarded as a bit of a white elephant. Not really the happy ending that anyone would want. And by happy ending, that means getting through the three months without ending up in hospital or jail.

There hadn't been too many stops at what most people would consider Europe's major tourist destinations, so spending a couple of days in Paris before catching the Eurostar back to London was acceptable. I wanted a place to settle, sort out luggage, and prepare mentally for going home. Finding an Airbnb studio near Père Lachaise Cemetery, I arrived in the city to a downpour. The journey from Nice was of no real consequence – it was on time and fast.

My host was Fidel, a jazz trombonist of some repute who handed me his keys, pointed me towards the list of information should I need to contact him and advised me of the best supermarket. Then he left. Parfait! It was a cosy studio with a tiny but oh so Parisian kitchen. Before this visit I had only spent a weekend in Paris with Steve, drinking mojitos, speaking in broad Dundonian to confuse everyone around us, and laughing – a lot. So outside of a few blocks of the Marais, Paris was still a place to be explored, but not on the first night.

The furthest I ventured was a fancy grocery store, with its confiture and fromage and interesting biscuits. The joy of bringing a bag of shopping back to a kitchen showed me that going home was going to be fine, in fact home was going to be bloody wonderful.

An evening of laundry, cooking, and looking at the photographs of the flat that was awaiting me in Dundee was blissful. There was no television, which stopped the magnetic pull of the sofa with its inevitable slack-jawed slump and flicking channels pretending to enjoy foreign TV, while for the love of god hoping to come across something decent in English.

There were two full days before an early Eurostar to London so plenty of time to satisfy my curiosity about a few things. The city didn't have a hold on me, so I decided to jump in with both feet to see the A-List sights that I had tried to avoid through the rest of the trip. The scale of the Eiffel Tower was surprising, particularly the vast expanse between its four legs, but there was no sense of being overwhelmed that this was something significant and inspiring. The lines to ascend the tower were long, the tat sellers, mostly of plastic towers for a Euro, were numerous and my desire to stick around zero. The Tower was more interesting from a distance, particularly as it proved to be a valuable landmark. Strolling through the back streets towards L'Arc de Triomphe then down the Champs d'Elysee showed how impressive the city is, but there was nothing here that was making my synapses crackle and my soul sing.

Once I had strolled through the Jardins des Tuileries and over to the Louvre, there was a quick tour of the museum shop. There was no need to queue for the gallery itself. There were thousands of Mona Lisas in here – on bags, cups, pencils, chocolate bars. She had even been blasted into a fake Andy Warhol… Ah, Leonardo you'd be inventing something to help artists spin in their graves to see this mass abuse of any work. It made Vienna's approach to Klimt look almost respectful. The night was spent at home, where there was a substantial dinner – I might have been a little over-zealous during the grocery shopping.

The next day in Paris had to have more meaning, so I had a stroll to the Marais. This was more like it. Heading to the banks of the Seine I spent not enough time but too much money on books at Shakespeare and Company. Following a day of much more charming streets and books and an incredible crêpe that managed to combine mushrooms, cheese, and an egg into something delicious, Paris could take me out for a drink but we wouldn't be going all the way yet. I would challenge anyone not to find their own Paris though, whether there is a tower involved or not.

Spending much of my final day in Montmartre, I had considered finding a wonderful Parisian restaurant to celebrate the last night of the trip, but the alone time was over. It was time to see people, and more than anything, it was time to laugh.

Paris had come with sleepless nights. There was no physical reason for this. The studio was warm, but not too warm. It was quiet and the bed comfortable. There was a dawning realisation that I was excited about going home. Not at all desperate for the journey to be over, but missing the people that meant so much to me. There would be one stop in London to catch up with Dawn and one night in Glasgow with Steve where I knew I'd laugh until my sides were sore. Finally it would back to Dundee to pick up the keys to a home that I hadn't seen apart from small photographs, and the exhilaration of having the chance to start again with three suitcases of belongings and a completely different outlook on life. It's no exaggeration to say that the three months had changed me. The physical changes might not be permanent. My weight would probably fluctuate over the seasons and years. The psychological changes were real and I knew they were lasting.

I felt no sadness boarding the Eurostar. It was the end of nothing and the beginning of everything.

UNPACKING

Once you have travelled, the voyage never ends but is
played out over and over again in the quietest chambers.
The mind can never break off from the journey.

Pat Conroy

We made it. Welcome home.

IF THE MAIN question before leaving was 'Why?' afterwards it was, 'Do you think you'll manage to settle?' There was a feeling that three months away would make those long-suffering feet eternally itchy, and now the only possible destiny was to ride the rails hobo-style, with nothing more than a spotted hankie on a stick.

Far from it. Embracing domesticity with the fervour of a 1950s housewife, the rented flat was furnished and made into a cosy nest within weeks. A place to plan and write and settle for a moment. Reconnecting with friends, of the two and four-legged variety, was also paramount.

The solo travel was valuable, although language barriers and cultural references meant laughing wasn't a huge part of the journey. It's also true that there weren't any acts of derring-do. There was no romance or even a wild, continental fling. It was three months in one life that passed in an unconventional but inspirational way.

On the many occasions of being completely lost, I didn't find myself; not that I was looking. I had the space and time to reassess priorities. Perhaps most importantly, by dealing with challenges and difficulties in a calm manner I learned to like myself and fill the well with some of that self-confidence that others had spoken of with such fervour.

Despite many sleepless nights, sunburns, bites, and general fatigue, friends have said that I look healthier and happier than ever before. It's true that I'm two stone lighter and have muscle definition in my legs like never before, but it's not about the physical. There's no doubt that the experience has shown me the value of exercise and prompted a new-found respect for cucumber. The difference is that self-respect means I now want to look after myself in the same way that I've always tried to look after other people and the pooches I love.

If you can indulge a wee bit of metaphor, the three months can be likened to the working on the side of the page when struggling to find the solution to a really hard sum. Not a bad result. And I saw a good bit of our fascinating, beautiful, diverse continent and managed to share it, not only now, but along the way. Sending postcards was important. We receive too many things through the letterbox that are brown and demanding, so a little colour from an exotic location can brighten a day. For me the effort of choosing the card, buying the stamps, writing the cards, and finding a post box was a joyous process, apart from in Romania (thanks Posta Romana), where it was impossible.

Our connection with things as ordinary as the post office is truly what brings a trip like this alive. It's not particularly about the exotic and artistic – sometimes it's about the things we know. Things that are seemingly so familiar can be seen through new eyes because of the small differences and the challenges they present.

Away from the tourist areas, observing how people get on with their day-to-day lives in supermarkets and on public transport is truly fascinating. Language can be irrelevant if there is a real desire to communicate, unfamiliar currencies are interesting and keep us on our toes, there's always the universal language of music and, too often today, the common bond of austerity.

At the time of writing, Europe has been changing. The refugee situation I witnessed has become known as the EU Refugee Crisis, with no real answer to what we can do for those fleeing Syria. The attacks on Paris and subsequent lockdowns of major cities have happened.

I hope this doesn't change Europe and those countries still looking to become part of the European Union. It's far from perfect, but the bonds are too important to break apart. I hope that my three months in 2015 wasn't the last summer of relative innocence for this fascinating, constantly evolving continent.

Scotland is home. There is absolutely no doubt about that now. However, like many other Scots, the travel bug is strong and there are still so many corners to explore – I'll be back. In sandals.

Hope to see you out there.

THE
DETAILS

the destinations

Brussels	Interlaken
Bruges	Montreux
Antwerp	Zurich
Rotterdam	Innsbruck
Breda	Vienna
Gouda	Brno
Utrecht	Cesky Krumlov
Haarlem	Prague
The Hague	Wroclaw
Texel – De Cocksdorp	Katowice
Oosterend	Bratislava
Oudenschilde	Košice
Den Burg	Eger
Groningen	Budapest
Bremen	Sighisoara
Eschede	Bucharest
Celle	Sofia
Hamburg	Nis (sort of)
Lübeck	Belgrade
Oslo	Zagreb
Bergen	Sarajevo
Aarhus	Split
Odense	Ancona
Copenhagen	Pedaso
Malmõ	Amandola
Norrköping	Florence
Stockholm	Genoa
Turku	Nice
Helsinki	Monaco
Lubeck	Beaulieu Sur Mer
Bern	Paris

the journeys

Dundee to Glasgow

Glasgow to London Euston

St Pancras to Brussels

Brussels to Bruges

Bruges to Antwerp

Antwerp to Rotterdam

Rotterdam to Breda

Breda to Rotterdam

Rotterdam to Gouda

Gouda to Utrecht

Utrecht to Amsterdam

Amsterdam to Haarlem

Haarlem to The Hague

The Hague to Haarlem

Haarlem to Alkmaar

Alkmaar to Amsterdam Sloterdijk

Amsterdam Sloterdijk
to Den Helder

Ferry – Den Helder to Texel

Texel Hopper bus
to De Cocksdorp

Texel Hopper bus from
Den Burg to De Cocksdorp

Ferry – Texel to Den Helder

Den Helder to Utrecht

Utrecht to Zwolle

Zwolle to Groningen

Groningen to Leer

Leer to Bremen

Bremen to Hannover

Hannover to Eschede

Eschede to Uelzen

Uelzen to Hamburg

Hamburg to Lübeck

Lübeck to Hamburg

Hamburg to Copenhagen

*(Train on ferry from Puttgarden,
Germany to Rødby, Denmark)*

Copenhagen to Gothenburg

Gothenburg to Oslo

Oslo to Bergen

Ferry – Bergen to Hirsthals
(Lilleheden) to Hjørring to Aarhus

Aarhus to Odense

Odense to Copenhagen

Copenhagen to Malmö

Malmö to Norrköping

Norrköping to Stockholm

Ferry – Stockholm to Turku

Turku to Helsinki

Ferry – Helsinki to
Lubeck/Travemunde

Lubeck to Hamburg

Hamburg to Basel

Basel to Olten

Olten to Bern

Bern to Interlaken

Interlaken to Bern

Bern to Lausanne

Lausanne to Montreux

Montreux to Lausanne

Lausanne to Bern

Bern to Zurich

Zurich to Innsbruck

Innsbruck to Vienna

Vienna to Brno

Brno to Ceske Budejovice

Ceske Budejovice to
Cesky Krumlov

Cesky Krumlov to
Ceske Budejovice

Ceske Budejovice to Prague

Prague to Usti Stad Norlice

Usti Stad Norlice to
Klodzko Glowne

Klodzko Glowne to
Wroclaw Glowny

Wroclaw Glowny to Katowice

Katowice to Breclav

Breclav to Bratislava

Bratislava to Košice

Košice to Miskolc

Miskolc to Füzesabony

Füzesabony to Eger

Eger to Fuezesabony

Fuezesabony to Budapest

Budapest to Sighisoara

Sighisoara to Bucharest

Bucharest to Sofia

Sofia to Nis

Nis to Belgrade

Belgrade to Zagreb

Zagreb to Sarajevo

Bus – Sarajevo to Split

Ferry – Split to Ancona

Ancona to Pedaso

Pedaso to Ancona

Ancona to Faenza

Faenza to Borgo San Lorenzo

Borgo San Lorenzo to Florence

Florence to Genoa

Genoa to Ventimiglia

Ventimiglia to Nice

Nice to Monaco

Monaco to Beaulieu Sur Mer

Beaulieu Sur Mer to Nice

Nice to Paris Gare de Lyon

Gare Du Nord to St Pancras

Euston to Glasgow

Glasgow to Dundee

the stats

Distance travelled: 18450 km, 11464 miles
Time travelled: 293 hours – 12 and-a-half days

the crowdfunders

Yvonne Bolouri

Gavin Gourlay

Alison Wallace

Phil Smith

Ewan Smith

Elaine Hirst

Juliet Smith

Jan Patience

Debra Costello

Ruth Ogilvie

Marney Keiller

Anne Everett-Ogston

Boo Paterson

Robert Haddock

Katie and Liam Brennan

Linda and Roddy Isles

Lindsay Duncan

Sean Guthrie

David Richards

Neil Forsyth

Dawn Schultz

Maggie Dun

Steve and Kat Paterson

Shenagh McAfee

Ali and Corrine Napier

Gary Clark

Shona Main and Nick Bruno

Caroline Stewart

Gordon Craigie

Angus Robb

Alison Burns

Maggie Ferrie, Paula Fenwick, and Patricia Fenwick

Alastair and Stella Brodie

Alan Wilson and Carol Larg

Alastair Jamieson

Colin and Mandip Sumby

Donna McManus

Audrey McCabe

Chae Strathie

Gillian Henney

Carolyn Lothian

Terry and Ross McCallum

Kirk Houston

Alison Brady

Euan Doig

Gillian Easson

Ronnie Gray

Maggie Ellis

Anna Day

Audrey McCabe

Kitty Finstad

Rosie Ivins and Sean Hamilton

Graeme Watt

Stewart Ross

Dave McDonald

Ross and Jacquie Turriff

Leon Strachan and Jacqui McGrath

Shona McKinnon Whitelaw

Marlyn Jeffrey

Shona and Frank Mills

Grant Ritchie

Aileen Lamb

Abby Lyons

Trish Webster

Kerin Bell

Shirley Wishart

Eileen McGinley

Theresa Talbot

Eddie Grady

Karen McDonell

Maureen Crosbie

David Somerville

Rolf Roscher and Felicity Steers

Robert and Trish McGlone

Donna Doogan

Barry Gibson

Jackie Brown

Jo Ahern

Nadine Stewart

John Collins

Dave McDonald

Stewart Ross

John Reilly

Paul Johnson

Jennie Patterson

Graeme Watt

Tim Dawson

Lynn Schreiber

Katrina Swanston

Robert Fyfe

Val Wilson

Liz and Peter Baillie

THE AUTHOR

Lorraine Wilson lives and works as a freelance writer from Dundee in Scotland. She is a former editor of The Scots Magazine. She really likes Jack Russell Terriers. At the time of writing she is still single.

Also by the Author

Take It To The Bridge – Dundee's Rock and Pop History
(Black & White Publishing, 2011)